VOICES OF RESISTANCE

VOICES OF RESISTANCE

Music, Femicide, and Gender Justice in Spain and Greece

BY

ANGELOS BOLLAS
Independent Scholar, Ireland

And

ALICIA CASTILLO VILLANUEVA
Dublin City University, Ireland

emerald PUBLISHING

United Kingdom – North America – Japan – India
Malaysia – China

Emerald Publishing Limited
Emerald Publishing, Floor 5, Northspring, 21-23 Wellington Street, Leeds LS1 4DL

First edition 2026

British Library Cataloguing in Publication Data
A catalogue record for this book is available from the British Library

ISBN: 978-1-83708-457-9 (Print)
ISBN: 978-1-83708-456-2 (Onlinc)
ISBN: 978-1-83708-458-6 (Epub)

For all victims of gender-based violence and femicide, and for those who continue to seek truth, remembrance and protection in their name. May their stories continue to resonate, urging us toward justice.

CONTENTS

ACKNOWLEDGEMENTS

We would like to thank Dr Sarah Meehan O'Callaghan and Jeremy Murphy from JM Agency for their expert editing services as well as all those who contributed in giving us time and space to think, write and produce this book. Alicia would like to thank Willie, Guillermo and David; Angelos would like to thank Apostolos. Finally, a special thanks to all the people in Emerald Publishing for their support with this project. A special mention to Daniel Ridge who believed in the idea that led to this book.

ABOUT THE BOOK

Voices of Resistance: Music, Femicide, and Gender Justice in Spain and Greece examines how feminist musical practices across Southern Europe confront femicide and gender-based violence through mourning, memory and political resistance. Drawing on detailed national case studies, the book argues that in contexts marked by institutional silences, legal gaps or patriarchal backlash, music becomes a crucial feminist tool for naming violence, honouring victims and sustaining collective demands for justice. In Spain, a rich genealogy of feminist musical activism, from María Jiménez's *Se acabó* to Rozalén's contemporary performances, intersects with a robust yet contested legislative landscape. These soundscapes function as emotional counterpublics that challenge antifeminist backlash and supplement the limitations of institutional responses. In Greece, where femicide lacks full legal recognition and media narratives often reproduce misogyny, music assumes an even more urgent role. Songs such as *Όλες απαντάμε αν αγγίξεις μία* and tributes to victims like Eleni Topaloudi transform public grief into mobilisation and forge affective publics that hold state and society accountable. Across both contexts, the book develops a shared analytic framework grounded in feminist theory, affect studies and sound studies. It demonstrates how music generates acoustic citizenship, forms transnational feminist resonances and sustains memory work that extends beyond the law. At the same time, it acknowledges the limits of cultural activism, highlighting tensions between visibility and structural change, the volatility of digital publics and the partial nature of affective justice. Ultimately, the book positions music as a vital yet incomplete mode of feminist world-making, capable of unsettling silence and imagining more just futures.

Keywords: Feminist musical activism; femicide; gender-based violence; affective publics; acoustic citizenship; memory and mourning; transnational feminist soundscapes; cultural resistance

1

RESONANT FUTURES: FEMINISM, MUSIC, AND THE SOUND OF JUSTICE

ABSTRACT

This introductory chapter situates Voices of Resistance: Music, Femicide, and Gender Justice in Southern Europe *within a comparative and transnational framework, examining how music in Spain and Greece has become a vital feminist response to femicide and gender-based violence. It outlines the book's central premise: that in contexts marked by patriarchal legacies, institutional failures and uneven legal protections, music operates as a political practice that names victims, mobilises emotions and creates spaces of civic witnessing. Through theoretical lenses from feminist studies, affect theory, sound studies and transnational feminism, this chapter conceptualises music as both testimony and resistance. It introduces key analytical tools, such as grievability, affective publics, acoustic citizenship and feminist soundscapes, to show how artists and activists transform mourning into collective action. It also positions Spain and Greece as parallel yet distinct case studies shaped by shared Mediterranean histories but divergent institutional trajectories, establishing the comparative foundations for the chapters that follow.*

Keywords: Femicide; feminist soundscapes; affective publics; Acoustic citizenship; mourning and memory; transnational feminism; gender-based violence

1. LISTENING AGAINST SILENCE

On a winter evening in Granada in December 2022, the Spanish singer Rozalén stood before an audience gathered to commemorate the 25th anniversary of the murder of Ana Orantes, whose televised testimony of domestic abuse in 1997, and subsequent killing by her ex-husband, shocked a nation into recognising gender-based violence as a social crisis. 'La puerta violeta' ['The Purple Door'] has now become an anthem of feminist resistance in Spain. The refrain echoed through the square as hundreds of women raised purple scarves, transforming the space of remembrance into one of defiance.

A few months later and across the Mediterranean, in Athens, dozens of women assembled in Syntagma Square to perform 'Όλες απαντάμε αν αγγίξεις μία' ('We All Respond if You Touch One'), a Greek adaptation of Vivir Quintana's Mexican feminist anthem 'Canción sin miedo' ('Song Without Fear'). The performers, members of the Open Orchestra collective, sang the names of murdered women: 'Με λένε Ανίσα, Καρολάιν και Ελένη' ('My name is Anisa, Caroline, and Eleni'). Their voices rose against the noise of city traffic, merging lament with accusation. Within hours, videos of the performance spread across social media under the hashtags #ΚαμίαΛιγότερη (*Not One Less*) and #NiUnaMenos, connecting Greece's struggle to a global feminist soundscape.

Both scenes capture the central concern of this book: how music in Southern Europe has become a vital arena for mourning, memory and resistance in response to femicide, the gender-motivated killing of women. The Canadian Femicide Observatory for Justice and Accountability (n.d.) explains that the term was first documented in John Corry's 1801 book *A Satirical View of London at the Commencement of the Nineteenth Century,* reintroduced by Diana E. H. Russell in 1976, and then expanded on again by her in 2012 to denote the structural, systemic nature of patriarchal violence. In contexts marked by institutional silence, legal gaps or political backlash, music performs the work that law and policy too often fail to do: it names, remembers and mobilises affective responses, bringing the unsaid into the realm of thought and feeling.

Spain and Greece, the two national case studies examined in this volume, occupy parallel yet distinct positions within the geography of European gender politics. Both are post-authoritarian societies, with Spain emerging from Francoism in 1975 and Greece from military dictatorship in 1974. In both countries, democratic renewal was accompanied by persistent patriarchal legacies. Both have witnessed an alarming escalation of gender-based killings since the late 1990s, even as feminist movements achieved unprecedented visibility, and in both, the cultural field, especially music, has become a resonant space where the collective demand for gender justice takes sonic form.

To listen to these songs is to hear more than melody. It is to encounter a form of civic testimony. When Rozalén sings for Ana Orantes or when the Open Orchestra chants the names of Eleni Topaloudi and Caroline Crouch, the act of singing transforms grief into political presence. As Judith Butler (2009) reminds us, public mourning can be a mode of resistance, an insistence that certain lives are 'grievable,' that their loss matters. In this sense, feminist music in Spain and Greece makes mourning audible and, in doing so, turns listening itself into an ethical and political act.

This book, *Voices of Resistance: Music, Femicide, and Gender Justice in Southern Europe*, begins from that premise. It listens to how artists, audiences and activists across the Mediterranean use sound to contest erasure and to weave emotional, cultural and political solidarity across borders. In amplifying these voices, the chapters that follow ask what it means to resist injustice and political oppression through music and what it means, equally, to listen.

2. CONCEPTUAL AND THEORETICAL FRAMEWORK

To understand how music participates in the struggle against gendered violence, we must first clarify the conceptual terrain of this book: the notion of femicide, the feminist frameworks that illuminate it and the theoretical approaches that help us interpret sound as a mode of political action.

2.1 Naming Femicide

The term femicide was first popularised by feminist sociologist Diana E. H. Russell, who used it in her 1976 testimony before the International Tribunal on Crimes against Women and later, with Jill Radford, defined it as 'the misogynist killing of women by men' (Radford & Russell, 1992, p. 3). While early usage focused on it being a form of lethal violence perpetrated by men against women, subsequent feminist scholarship, particularly from Latin America, expanded the term's meaning. Marcela Lagarde y de los Ríos (2006) introduced *feminicidio* to describe not only individual acts of murder but also the state and societal complicity that allow such crimes to continue with impunity. For Lagarde, femicide signifies a *political crime*, a symptom of structural inequality, institutional neglect and patriarchal control.

In Europe, legal frameworks remain uneven. Spain recognises *violencia de género* (gender-based violence) within intimate relationships, codified in the Organic Law 1/2004 on Integrated Protection Measures Against Gender Violence (LOMPIVG). In contrast, Greece, despite ratifying the Istanbul Convention in 2018, has yet to enshrine femicide as a distinct legal category. These gaps reveal a *geography of impunity*, an uneven global cartography in which the same crime is differently named, measured and mourned. It is within this landscape of partial recognition that culture, and especially music, assumes political urgency. When law remains silent, song speaks.

2.2 Feminist and Cultural Frameworks

The chapters in this book draw from feminist cultural theory, which situates artistic production as a field of political struggle. We view representation as the space where power and pleasure converge (Meyrowitz, 2008) and emphasise that culture is never merely reflective but constitutive of social reality (Mukherjee, 1998). Sara Ahmed's (2010) work on affect and feminism highlights how emotions such as anger, grief and hope *stick* to bodies and circulate through communities, generating political attachments. In the songs examined here, affect is not an individual response but a *shared orientation*, a means by which listeners recognise one another as participants in a collective demand for justice.

Within this framework, music functions as feminist praxis. It translates affect into action and emotion into mobilisation. As Tia DeNora (2000) argues, music *affords* social agency by structuring how people feel and act together. It does not simply express political sentiment. It organises it, shaping rhythms of protest and patterns of solidarity. These insights align with Judith Butler's (2009) theorisation of performativity and public assembly: collective acts of voice and gesture, from singing to marching, constitute the very fabric of political subjectivity. When women sing the names of victims, Ana, Eleni and Caroline, they enact a politics of the body in alliance, transforming vulnerability into collective strength.

2.3 Sound Studies and Acoustic Citizenship

From the perspective of sound studies, music's political power lies not only in lyrics but in *listening itself. Acoustic citizenship* is enacted as the practice of claiming social and political belonging through acts of sounding and hearing

(Sonevytsky, 2019). Sound travels across boundaries, linguistic, spatial and affective, creating communities that are felt as much as they are understood. Zizi Papacharissi's (2015) notion of *affective publics* complements this idea. In the digital age, emotions circulate through media networks, transforming listening into a participatory, connective experience.

In the context of gender justice, this means that when audiences share, stream or perform feminist songs, they engage in what Nancy Fraser (1990) termed *subaltern counterpublics*, alternative spheres of discourse where marginalised voices gain resonance. The 'public' formed by the listening ear is no less political than the one formed by the voting hand; both enact citizenship, but the former operates through empathy and resonance rather than representation.

2.4 A Transnational Feminist Lens

Finally, this book approaches Spain and Greece through a transnational feminist lens (Alvarez et al., 2014; Mohanty, 2013), recognising that while the political contexts differ, the emotional and cultural grammars of resistance are profoundly interconnected. The feminist anthem 'Ni una menos', which originated in Argentina, the Mexican 'Canción sin Miedo,' and their Southern European echoes demonstrate how sound traverses borders, carrying both solidarity and specificity.

By tracing how Spanish and Greek artists localise global feminist repertoires, *Voices of Resistance* situates Southern Europe within a wider network of feminist cultural activism. These cross-border resonances remind us that resistance is not only spoken but sung and that, in song, the struggle for justice becomes both collective and continuous.

3. COMPARATIVE FRAMEWORK: SPAIN AND GREECE

3.1 Shared Geographies of Patriarchy

Spain and Greece occupy parallel positions in the European imagination: Mediterranean, post-dictatorial societies that transitioned to democracy in the mid-1970s and integrated into the European Union during the 1980s. Both countries share complex legacies of authoritarianism, Catholic or Orthodox conservatism, and familial patriarchy, each of which continues to shape gender relations. As scholars such as Silvia Walby (2003) and

Valiente Fernández (2006) have noted, patriarchal systems are resilient precisely because they adapt to democratic modernity, reappearing in the gaps between law, culture and everyday life.

In both Spain and Greece, the family has historically functioned as the primary site of moral order and social control, an institution sanctified by religion and protected by the state. During Francoist Spain (1939–1975) and the Greek military junta (1967–1974), women were legally and ideologically subordinated to male authority: confined to domestic roles, denied full autonomy and represented as guardians of purity and nationhood (Avdela, 1997; Moreno-Seco, 2015). Even after the transitions to democracy, cultural continuities persisted. Public discourse may have embraced equality, yet patriarchal norms continued to govern affective and domestic life, naturalising control, jealousy and possession as forms of love.

This shared cultural inheritance provides the backdrop for the persistence of gender-based violence. The murder of Ana Orantes in Spain (1997) and of Eleni Topaloudi in Greece (2018) each marked national turning points, rupturing the illusion that such violence belonged to the private sphere. Yet, their aftermaths reveal divergent institutional trajectories: one of legal consolidation and the other of cultural resistance.

3.2 Spain: From Legal Reform to Cultural Mobilisation

Spain has often been cited as a European pioneer in gender-violence legislation. The Organic Law 1/2004 on LOMPIVG established a comprehensive framework that recognised gender violence as structural, mandated educational prevention and created specialised courts and victim support services (Bodelón, 2014). Subsequent measures, such as the 2017 State Pact against Gender Violence, expanded the law's scope to include sexual, economic and vicarious violence while the Comprehensive Guarantee of Sexual Freedom Law (Ley del 'Solo Sí es Sí,' 2022) placed consent at the heart of sexual crime legislation.

Yet even as these legal advances positioned Spain as a model of gender equality, cultural and political tensions intensified. The far-right Vox party has repeatedly sought to dismantle or dilute gender-violence laws, framing them as 'ideological' or 'discriminatory against men' (Cabezas Fernández, 2023). This backlash, amplified by digital misinformation, is the manifestation of an *ambivalence of progress* (Volpe, 2025); that is, each gain in recognition of equality produces a counter-movement aimed at restoring patriarchal order.

It is precisely within this climate that music became a site of feminist counter-discourse. From María Jiménez's flamenco anthem 'Se acabó' in the late 1970s to Rozalén's contemporary ballads and the feminist collectives of *Mujeres Artistas contra la Violencia de Género*, Spanish artists have translated legislative abstraction into lived emotion. Music rehumanises what law bureaucratises, giving voice to the affective dimensions of gender justice and sustaining feminist momentum amid political contestation.

3.3 Greece: Legal Silence and Cultural Resonance

In contrast, Greece presents a case of cultural activism compensating for institutional inertia. Although the country ratified the Council of Europe's Istanbul Convention in 2018, it has yet to adopt femicide as a legal category. Gender-based killings are prosecuted under general homicide laws, obscuring their systemic nature (Kyriakopoulou-Kollia, 2019). Feminist organisations such as Diotima Centre and Women's Rights Network have documented dozens of such cases each year, noting persistent failures in police response, judicial sensitivity and media framing (Kourou & Athanasiades, 2022).

Mainstream media have often reproduced victim-blaming narratives, portraying perpetrators as jealous lovers or psychologically unstable and victims as careless or provocative (Papagiannopoulou, 2022). The cumulative effect has been a cultural silencing that feminist collectives have sought to rupture through art, protest and song. Street demonstrations following the murders of Eleni Topaloudi (2018) and Caroline Crouch (2021) transformed grief into collective performance, echoing slogans such as 'Δεν ήταν η ζήλια· ήταν η πατριαρχία' ('It wasn't jealousy; it was patriarchy').

In this context, music has emerged as both memorial and manifesto. Songs like 'Όλες απαντάμε αν αγγίξεις μία' ('We All Respond if You Touch One') (2022) and 'Ελένη Τοπαλούδη' ('Eleni Topaloudi') (2021) do not simply accompany activism; they *constitute* it. They name the dead, indict the system and invite listeners to join a *community of hearing* (Garcia & Vemuri, 2017). Through melody and repetition, these songs build *affective publics* (Papacharissi, 2015), digital and physical collectives bonded by shared emotion and moral outrage. In Greece, where political and media institutions often fail to articulate feminist perspectives, the cultural sphere has become a surrogate parliament of voices.

3.4 Convergences and Contrasts

Juxtaposing Spain and Greece reveals both common struggles and complementary strengths. Spain demonstrates the potential of institutionalising feminist gains but also the fragility of such achievements under populist attack. Greece exposes the dangers of legal omission but illustrates how culture can mobilise moral consensus from below.

Both contexts underscore the role of music as connective tissue between law, culture and emotion. Whether amplifying existing frameworks (as in Spain) or substituting for absent ones (as in Greece), music performs a democratic function: it creates spaces of listening where official discourse falters. Across both nations, the feminist soundscape resists erasure, insisting that justice must be heard as well as seen.

4. MUSIC, MEMORY AND RESISTANCE

4.1 From Witnessing to Remembering

In contexts of persistent gender violence, *memory* becomes a political battleground. Feminist theorists have long recognised that remembrance is never neutral. It determines whose suffering is acknowledged and whose remains invisible. Elizabeth Jelin (1998) describes memory as a *terrain of struggle* where competing actors vie to define the meaning of past trauma. Within Southern Europe, where both Spain and Greece experienced long periods of dictatorship, memory work has historically been tied to political violence and national reconciliation. Yet in recent years, a new archive of memory has emerged, one centred not on political prisoners or martyrs but on the women murdered in their homes, streets and workplaces.

This shift signals the emergence of what Marianne Hirsch (2008) calls *postmemory*: a collective practice through which those who did not directly experience violence nevertheless inherit its affective weight. When contemporary musicians sing the names of Ana Orantes, Eleni Topaloudi or Caroline Crouch, they participate in a *postmemory of femicide*. Their songs invite listeners to inhabit grief that is not individually theirs, transforming mourning into an act of solidarity. The sound becomes a conduit through which private loss acquires public resonance.

4.2 The Sound of Collective Mourning

Music has long been intertwined with ritual, commemoration and protest. As Tia DeNora (2000) argues, it structures emotional experience, turning feeling into form. In Spain and Greece, feminist musicians use melody and repetition to perform what Judith Butler (2009) terms the *politics of grievability*: the assertion that women's deaths matter and that they demand recognition rather than erasure.

The Greek song 'Όλες απαντάμε αν αγγίξεις μία' ('We All Respond if You Touch One', adapted from Vivir Quintana's Mexican 'Canción sin miedo", exemplifies this process. By naming victims aloud, '*Με λένε Ανίσα, Καρολάιν και Ελένη*' ('My name is Anisa, Caroline, and Eleni'), the song transforms statistics into stories. Each repetition constitutes an act of defiance against institutional forgetting. The same holds true for Foivos Delivorias's 'Eleni Topaloudi' (2021), which reclaims a sensationalised media case as a solemn elegy, repositioning the listener from voyeur to witness.

In Spain, artists such as Rozalén, Cristina del Valle and Pasión Vega similarly use music to bridge mourning and mobilisation. Their performances at commemorative events, such as Rozalén's 2022 tribute to Ana Orantes, turn remembrance into activism, linking personal pain to collective demand. Pierre Nora (1989) suggests that cultural artefacts become sites of memory when they anchor emotion to space and time. In this sense, these songs function as *aural memorials* – sonic monuments that circulate through radio, concerts and digital media, ensuring that the victims' voices persist in the public ear.

4.3 Memory, Transmission and the Digital Sphere

The circulation of feminist music today depends heavily on digital infrastructures. Online platforms such as YouTube, Instagram and Spotify have transformed songs into transnational tools of mobilisation. Zizi Papacharissi's (2015) *affective publics* captures this dynamic: emotions travel across networks, linking listeners into ephemeral yet powerful communities of feeling. Each share, remix or repost of a feminist song extends its life, turning sound into a renewable form of protest.

In this digital ecology, listening becomes participation. When users replay Rozalén's 'La puerta violeta' or the Open Orchestra's performance on March 8, they join a *community of resonance,* a dispersed collective bound not by proximity but by shared affect. This participatory listening is central to what we might call *digital acoustic citizenship*: an enactment of civic belonging through sonic engagement.

Moreover, these digital traces accumulate to form a living feminist archive. Unlike institutional archives, which fix meaning through documentation, the sonic archive is fluid, recursive and affective. It evolves with each new performance, each new act of listening. The chorus '*Ni una menos*,' echoed in Spanish, Greek and Italian adaptations, becomes not only a slogan but an *auditory commons*, that is a shared space of empathy that transcends linguistic and national boundaries.

4.4 Resistance Through Aesthetics

If mourning provides the emotional foundation of feminist music, *resistance* gives it direction. As Angela Davis (2020) observes in her reflections on protest music, art cannot by itself create social change, but it can generate the affects and imaginaries, both cultural and individual, through which change becomes thinkable. In both Spain and Greece, feminist musicians blend traditional genres, *flamenco*, *copla* and *entechno*, with contemporary idioms such as pop, rap and punk to destabilise the patriarchal narratives embedded within national culture.

The feminist reappropriation of these forms transforms them into tools of critique. Flamenco, once associated with the romanticised suffering of women, becomes a language of defiance in María Jiménez's 'Se acabó' ('It's over,' 1978). In Greece, the *mirologi* (lament), historically confined to women's domestic mourning, re-emerges in songs like Orestis Dandtos's 'Τακούνια για Καρφιά' ('Heels for Nails,' 2023) as a public act of rage. These transformations echo Jacques Rancière's (2009) notion of the *politics of aesthetics*: the reordering of the sensible and the redistribution of what can be heard, seen and felt. Feminist musicians alter not only content but perception – teaching societies to listen differently.

Through this aesthetic politics, music becomes a form of witnessing that is also a form of world-making. It bridges the personal and the political, grief and agency, silence and speech. Its power lies precisely in this oscillation: a song can weep and protest simultaneously.

4.5 The Ethics of Listening

If feminist music transforms mourning into resistance, it also demands a new ethics of listening. As Michael Chion (2012) reminds us, listening is never passive; it is interpretive, selective and embodied. To listen to a song about feminicide is to encounter the pain of others and to decide whether that pain will move us to action.

An ethical listener, as Sara Ahmed (2010) might argue, is one who allows discomfort to register, who refuses to turn away from the unsettling sound of suffering. In this sense, feminist protest music in Spain and Greece trains listeners in attentiveness to history, to injustice, and to the ongoing struggle for gender justice. The act of hearing becomes a practice of solidarity, a way of holding space for lives that patriarchal structures would prefer to forget.

Together, these dynamics, memory, mourning, aesthetic resistance and ethical listening compose the soundscape of feminist activism in Southern Europe. They illustrate how music operates as both archive and horizon, preserving the memory of violence while imagining futures grounded in equality and care.

5. STRUCTURE AND CONTRIBUTION OF THE BOOK

This book, *Voices of Resistance: Music, Femicide, and Gender Justice in Spain and Greece*, is composed of two main chapters that together trace the emergence of a feminist sonic politics across Spain and Greece. Although the chapters stand independently as national case studies, they are designed to be read dialogically. Each explores how women artists, activists and publics have mobilised music to confront gender-based violence, and together they reveal a shared Mediterranean soundscape of mourning and defiance.

The first chapter, '"Not One More": Music, Memory, and the Struggle for Gender Justice in Spain', situates the Spanish experience of gender-based violence within a historical and political continuum that begins with the 1997 murder of Ana Orantes. This event marked a rupture in Spanish public consciousness and inaugurated a new era of feminist activism. The chapter follows the trajectory from that moment to the contemporary feminist movement, examining how legislative advances, such as the Organic Law 1/2004 on LOMPIVG and later reforms, coexisted with enduring social inequalities and, more recently, with the reactionary rhetoric of the far right. Through analyses of artists including María Jiménez, Cristina del Valle, Rozalén and genres such as female *perreo*, the chapter demonstrates how music has served as a pedagogical and political tool, transforming personal testimony into collective awareness. Feminist musicians, Castillo Villanueva argues, have not only narrated women's suffering but have also educated audiences, mobilised emotion and sustained the memory of victims in the face of institutional complacency. In doing so, they have turned the cultural sphere into a vital site of public accountability and feminist pedagogy.

The second chapter, 'Sounding the Alarm: The Role of Music in Shaping Public Discourse on Femicides in Greece', turns to a different yet complementary context. In Greece, where femicide has yet to be recognised as a legal category, the struggle for recognition has taken place largely through cultural and affective means. Centring on emblematic cases such as those of Eleni Topaloudi (2018) and Caroline Crouch (2021), the chapter shows how musicians and feminist collectives have transformed mourning into mobilisation. Through close readings of contemporary songs, including 'Όλες απαντάμε αν αγγίξεις μία' ('We All Respond if You Touch One'), Foivos Delivorias's 'Ελένη Τοπαλούδη', and Orestis Dandtos's 'Τακούνια για Καρφιά' ('Heels for Nails'), the chapter develops the concept of *acoustic citizenship*, a form of political belonging and participation enacted through sound and listening. Here, music compensates for institutional absence: it names victims, exposes systemic injustice and fosters solidarity among listeners who, through acts of hearing and sharing, form *affective publics* (Papacharissi, 2015). In a society where the judiciary and media often reproduce patriarchal norms, music becomes a counter-public sphere in which grief and anger are organised into collective expression.

Together, these chapters trace a continuum of feminist sound across Southern Europe. Spain exemplifies a context where feminist progress has been institutionalised through law but remains contested by political backlash; Greece illustrates how, in the absence of comprehensive legal recognition, culture becomes the principal medium of feminist resistance. In both cases, music emerges as a bridge between the personal and the political, between mourning and mobilisation. It functions as connective tissue linking legislation, activism and emotional life, reminding us that social transformation depends as much on how societies *feel* as on how they legislate.

Methodologically, the book adopts a comparative and interdisciplinary approach, integrating feminist theory, cultural sociology and musicology. It treats music not merely as artistic expression but as a form of social text, an intermedial practice where emotion, politics and cultural memory converge. Attention is given both to the lyrical content of songs and to their social circulation: how they are performed, received and shared across digital and physical spaces. This approach aligns with intersectional feminism's insistence on examining how structures of power, patriarchy, religion, nationalism and class intersect to shape both the production of art and the experience of violence. It also draws upon affect theory and sound studies to illuminate how music organises feeling and enables listening as citizenship (Watson et al., 2014).

The book's contribution lies in its proposal that feminist music in Southern Europe constitutes a new form of political practice, an *aural feminism* (Malekpour, 2022) that operates through emotion, memory and resonance. By attending to the sonic dimensions of gender justice, it expands feminist scholarship beyond the visual and textual to the acoustic. It shows how listening, often dismissed as passive, can itself be an act of resistance, a means of recognising suffering and reaffirming collective responsibility. At the same time, it contributes to European gender studies by situating Spain and Greece within global feminist movements, revealing how transnational exchanges, from *Ni Una Menos* to 'Canción sin miedo', are reinterpreted through local histories and musical traditions.

In this sense, *Voices of Resistance* speaks both to scholars and to practitioners. It invites readers to reconsider music not simply as accompaniment to protest but as protest itself: a medium through which women reclaim narrative authority, mourn the dead and demand justice. The chapters that follow listen to these acts of resistance as they unfold in melody, rhythm and voice, proposing that the pursuit of gender justice requires not only new laws and institutions but also new ways of hearing one another.

6. CLOSING VISION: TOWARDS A POLITICS OF LISTENING

When women sing the names of the dead, they do not merely remember; they call the living to account. Across Spain and Greece, and throughout the transnational networks that connect them, music has become the pulse of feminist resistance: a medium through which silence is broken, pain is shared and justice is imagined. To listen to these songs is to participate in an act of witnessing that refuses erasure. It is to acknowledge that the stories of Ana, Eleni, Caroline and countless others are not isolated tragedies but echoes of the same structural violence that reverberates across borders, languages and generations.

This book begins from the conviction that listening is political. In the struggle against gender-based violence, listening entails far more than passively hearing words or melodies. It is the ethical labour of actively attending to voices long dismissed or drowned out. It demands that we stay with discomfort, that we allow grief and anger to unsettle the normality that sustains patriarchy and that we listen for the silences in our own capacity to hear. Feminism often begins with the moment one becomes *out of tune* with the world. Music makes that dissonance audible, giving it rhythm and form. Through its capacity to move and connect, sound teaches us that solidarity is not only spoken but felt.

The songs examined in *Voices of Resistance* transform listening into a shared civic practice. They create *acoustic communities* (Foreman, 2011), spaces where people recognise one another through resonance rather than resemblance. These communities are fragile yet profound: they do not require agreement, only attention. When Rozalén sings for Ana Orantes in Granada, when the Open Orchestra chants the names of Greek victims in Syntagma Square and when Foivos Delivorias records 'Eleni Topaloudi', each performance becomes a temporary republic of voices, a fleeting democracy of sound. Within these moments, music achieves what institutions often fail to: it restores dignity, insists on visibility and gestures towards collective healing.

To imagine gender justice in Southern Europe, then, is to imagine a politics of listening, one that values resonance over rhetoric, empathy over authority. It is to recognise that law, policy and activism must be sustained by emotional infrastructures capable of hearing the human consequences of inequality. Music, with its capacity to carry memory, to transmit affect, and to assemble communities, provides one such infrastructure. It turns mourning into a method for justice and empathy into endurance.

As the chapters that follow will show, the feminist soundscapes of Spain and Greece are not merely artistic responses to violence; they are political instruments through which societies rehearse alternative futures. To listen to them attentively is to hear the possibility of a different social order, one grounded not in domination but in care, not in silence but in solidarity.

This book invites its readers to join in that listening.

REFERENCES

Ahmed, S. (2010). *The promise of happiness*. Duke University Press.

Alvarez, S.E., de Lima Costa, C., Feliu, V., Hester, R., Klahn, N., & Thayer, M. (Eds) (2014), *Translocalities/translocalidades: Feminist politics of translation in the Latin/a Americas*. Duke University Press.

Avdela, E. (1997). Contested meanings: Protection and resistance in labour inspectors' reports in twentieth-century Greece. *Gender & History*, *9*(2), pp. 310–332.

Bodelón, E. (2014). Violencia institucional y violencia de género. *Anales de la Cátedra Francisco Suárez*, *48*, 131–155. https://doi.org/10.30827/acfs.v48i0.2783

Butler, J. (2009). *Frames of war: When is life grievable?* Verso Books.

Cabezas Fernández, A. (2023). *La reacción patriarcal: Saberes críticos y feministas ante el autoritarismo global.* Bellaterra.

Canadian Femicide Observatory for Justice and Accountability. (n.d.). *History of the term femicide.* https://femicideincanada.ca/what-is-femicide/history/

Chion, M. (2012). The three listening modes. In J. Sterne (Ed), *The sound studies reader* (pp. 48–53). Routledge.

Davis, A. Y. (2020). Struggle, solidarity, and social change. In *The Routledge handbook of the politics of the# MeToo movement* (pp. 27–33). Routledge.

DeNora, T. (2000). *Music in everyday life.* Cambridge University Press.

Foreman, I. (2011). Uncanny soundscapes: Towards an inoperative acoustic community. *Organised Sound*, *16*(3), 264–271.

Fraser, N. (1990). Rethinking the public sphere: A contribution to the critique of actually existing democracy. *Social Text*, *25/26*, 56–80.

Garcia, C. K., & Vemuri, A. (2017). Girls and young women resisting rape culture through YouTube videos. *Girlhood Studies*, *10*(2), 26–44.

Hirsch, M. (2008). The generation of postmemory. *Poetics Today*, *29*(1), 103–128.

Jelin, E. (1998). *Toward a culture of participation and citizenship: Challenges for a more equitable world.* In A. Escobar, S. Alvarez, & E. Dagnino (Eds), *Cultures of politics/politics of cultures* (pp. 405–414). Westview Press.

Kourou, M., & Athanasiades, C. (2022). The portrayal of femicide in the Greek internet press. *Scientific Annals-School of Psychology AUTh*, *14*, 173–200.

Kyriakopoulou-Kollia, F. (2019). *A feminist criminological critique of aspects of the criminal justice system and the whole-system response towards female victims of intimate partner abuse* [Doctoral dissertation, Newcastle University]. University Repository. http://theses.ncl.ac.uk/jspui/handle/10443/4734

Lagarde, M. (2006). Introduction. In D. E. Russell & R. A. Harmes (Eds), *Feminicidio: Una perspectiva global* (pp. 11–42). Unam.

Malekpour, M. (2022). The cultural dialogue of fidelity and rendering in the music of Googoosh in Hamsafar (1975). *Resonance: The Journal of Sound and Culture*, *3*(4), 379–393.

Meyrowitz, J. (2008). Power, pleasure, patterns: Intersecting narratives of media influence. *Journal of Communication*, *58*(4), 641–663.

Mohanty, C. T. (2013). *Feminism without borders: Decolonising theory, practicing solidarity*. Duke University Press.

Moreno-Seco, M. (2015). Partido Comunista y feminismo. *Vingtième Siècle - Revue d'Histoire*, *126*(2), 133–146.

Mukherjee, R. (1998). Social reality and culture. *Current Sociology*, *46*(2), 39–50.

Nora, P. (1989). Between memory and history: Les lieux de mémoire. *Representations*, 7–24.

Papacharissi, Z. (2015). *Affective publics: Sentiment, technology, and politics*. Oxford University Press.

Papagiannopoulou, M. (2022). *Gender-based violence in the pandemic period*. Centre for Gender Studies.

Radford, J., & Russell, D. (Eds). (1992). *Femicide: The politics of woman killing*. Twayne Publishers.

Rancière, J. (2009). Contemporary art and the politics of aesthetics. In *Communities of sense: Rethinking aesthetics and politics* (pp. 31–50).

Sonevytsky, M. (2019). *Wild music: Sound and sovereignty in Ukraine*. Wesleyan University Press.

Valiente Fernández, C. (2006). *El feminismo de Estado en España: El Instituto de la Mujer (1983–2003)*. Universitat de València.

Volpe, A. (2025). *Progress, self-criticism, and normativity* (pp. 1–14). Critical Horizons.

Walby, S. (2003). *Gender transformations*. Routledge.

Watson, V. W., Knight, M. G., & Jaffee, A. T. (2014). Beyond# talking and# texting: African immigrant youth's social–civic literacies and negotiations of citizenship across participatory new media technologies. *Citizenship Teaching & Learning*, *10*(1), 43–62.

2

'NOT ONE MORE': MUSIC, MEMORY AND THE STRUGGLE FOR GENDER JUSTICE IN SPAIN

ABSTRACT

This chapter examines how music in Spain has become a powerful medium for confronting gender-based violence and feminicide, tracing its evolution from the late Franco dictatorship to the digital present. It explores how songs by artists such as María Jiménez, Rozalén and contemporary urban performers transform individual experiences of pain and resistance into collective soundscapes of feminist memory. Drawing on feminist, memory and affect theories (Jelin, Hirsch, Ahmed, Butler) together with performance and resonance approaches (Taylor, Rigney), the chapter conceptualises listening as an ethical and political act that mediates between mourning and mobilisation. Set against Spain's socio-legal framework – marked by the 2004 Gender Violence Act, successive reforms and sustained feminist activism – it highlights how music amplifies social awareness while exposing the limits of institutional responses. Despite significant legal and cultural progress, feminicides persist, revealing the need for affective and cultural forms of justice beyond the law. By analysing genres from flamenco and pop to reggaetón and digital activism, the chapter argues that feminist music functions as both testimony and reparation, transforming grief into resonance. Ultimately, it presents music as a living archive of gender justice, where memory, affect and activism converge to sustain resistance and hope.

Keywords: Femicide in Spain; feminist memory; protest music; feminist musical activism; cultural justice; listening as political practice; affective politics; gender-based violence

1. INTRODUCTION: MUSIC, MEMORY AND FEMINICIDE – A TURNING POINT IN SPANISH GENDER-BASED VIOLENCE AWARENESS

Spanish society began to become aware of gender-based violence after the murder of Ana Orantes in 1997. Desperate due to her husband's abuse and the lack of support from public institutions, she publicly denounced his violence on the television programme *De tarde en tarde* (a late-afternoon regional talk show broadcast by Canal Sur). A mother of eight and sixty years old at the time, Ana appeared on the show a year after her divorce, detailing the abuse she had endured during 40 years of marriage and even after their separation. She was the first woman in Spain to publicly speak out about the physical and psychological abuse she had suffered at the hands of her husband. Thirteen days after her appearance, on 17 December 1997, Ana Orantes was brutally burned alive by her ex-husband (Gordillo de Paz & Manganas, 2025).

Following Spain's long dictatorship (1939–1975), divorce was legalised in 1981, but Ana's husband successfully convinced the court to deny her request for separation. Even after her eventual divorce, Ana was forced to share a home with her abuser, as recommended by a local judge. Her story brought to light the suffering and cruelty endured by hundreds of women across the country. At the time, the press reported that Ana was the 60th woman killed by gender-based violence that year (El País, 1997) although Spain had yet to begin collecting official data on what are now known as feminicides – the gender-motivated killing of women, often marked by impunity. While the term 'feminicide' is widely used in Latin America and internationally, in Spain, these killings are officially recorded under *violencia de género* (gender-based violence), a legal category focused primarily on intimate partner or ex-partner violence.

On 17 December 2022, the singer Rozalén's music closed a tribute to Ana Orantes in Granada, who had been murdered 25 years earlier. The visibly moved singer stated that this killing had 'left a deep mark' on her, as it had happened when she was only 11 years old (Arroyo, 2022). This feminicide, which shocked Spanish society enormously, contributed significantly to changing public perceptions regarding the issue of gender-based violence.

The murder of Ana Orantes signalled a turning point in Spanish society's awareness and response to gender violence. It exposed the systemic failures of legal and social institutions in protecting victims and sparked a wave of public outrage and activism. In 1999, singer Cristina del Valle founded the *Plataforma de Mujeres Artistas contra la Violencia de Género* (Platform of Women

Artists Against Gender Violence), one of the first coordinated feminist initiatives that brought together artists and activists. This mobilisation contributed to increasing the visibility of gender violence in public discourse and to consolidating a broader social movement around the issue. The platform aimed to raise awareness and sensitise the public about the realities of gender violence while also serving as a political pressure group demanding comprehensive legal reforms (Del Valle, 1999). Despite these growing demands, the conservative *Partido Popular* (People's Party, PP), led by Prime Minister José María Aznar, who won the 2000 elections, largely ignored calls for legislative action. It was only after the socialist government under José Luis Rodríguez Zapatero took office that the Ley de Medidas de Protección Integral contra la Violencia de Género (Organic Law on Integrated Protection Measures against Gender Violence (LOMPIVG) was passed in 2004, establishing a comprehensive framework for victim protection, prevention and prosecution.

This chapter explores how music – especially through the voices of female singers – has served as a powerful tool to confront gender-based violence and feminicide in Spain. It traces the political, social and cultural changes following the Orantes case, illustrating how music has been employed as a form of expression, resistance and protest. Furthermore, it analyses how musical genres and feminist movements have intersected to create spaces for social critique and activism. Drawing on feminist, memory and affect theories (Jelin, Hirsch, Ahmed, Butler) together with performance and resonance approaches (Taylor, Rigney), the chapter examines the narrative, sonic and performative dimensions of selected artists and their songs. These songs function as sites of public mourning and collective grieving, enabling society to process trauma and exposing the limits of institutional responses. In this way, musical expression contributes significantly to the construction of feminist memory and the mobilisation of political activism against gender-based violence.

Importantly, the chapter situates 'feminicide' both in its local Spanish legal context and within a broader, international feminist framework. While Spain's legal system focuses on gender-based violence targeting intimate partners, the term 'feminicide' encompasses a wider spectrum of gender-related killings and structural impunity – first introduced by Diana E. H. Russell at the *International Tribunal on Crimes Against Women* (1976) and later developed with Jill Radford in *Femicide: The Politics of Woman Killing* (1992). Subsequently, Marcela Lagarde (2005) redefined the term as *feminicidio* within Latin American feminist theory, exposing not only individual acts of violence but also the systemic patriarchal structures and state complicity that enable and perpetuate such crimes.

The title of this chapter, 'Not One More', echoes the feminist slogan '*Ni una más*' – a rallying cry that emerged in Spanish-speaking feminist movements in response to the alarming rise in gender-related killings of women. Popularised particularly in Latin America through the movement Ni Una Menos ('Not One Woman Less'), the phrase has also resonated widely in Spain as both a form of public grief and a powerful call for justice. While women's voices have historically been muted, this chapter frames music as a form of resistance that simultaneously channels feminist memory and articulates collective demands for justice.

The discussion unfolds in seven sections. Following this introduction, Section 2 traces the emergence of gender violence as a public and political concern in Spain, examining the legal, institutional and cultural transformations that have shaped the country's response since the democratic transition. It situates the case of Ana Orantes and subsequent reforms within broader debates on state responsibility, feminist mobilisation and the challenges posed by the far-right backlash. Section 3 reviews existing scholarship on music, feminism and gender-violence, identifying how sound and song have been mobilised as tools of protest, testimony and collective healing. It underscores the scarcity of sustained analyses of music as a site of feminist memory and cultural justice, thereby establishing the basis for an interdisciplinary approach. Section 4 traces the genealogy of feminist sound in Spain from the 1970s to the 1990s, exploring early expressions of resistance in songs by Mari Trini and María Jiménez and the subversive aesthetics of the Movida Madrileña. Section 5 focuses on the affective and collective dimensions of music in the 2000s and 2010s, analysing how feminist anthems such as 'La Puerta Violeta' ['The Purple Door'] and the chants of the 8M (8 March) strikes transformed grief into collective mobilisation. Section 6 turns to contemporary reconfigurations, examining digital feminism, reggaetón and urban sound practices that reclaim pleasure and embodiment as spaces of agency and justice, culminating in the resonance of 'Se acabó' ['It's Over'] as a transgenerational anthem. Finally, Section 7 concludes by reflecting on how feminist music in Spain makes violence audible and transforms listening itself into an ethical and political practice of remembrance and gender justice.

By centring the role of music in the struggle against gender-based violence, the chapter shows how cultural production complements – and often challenges – institutional forms of justice. Music, as an emotional and accessible medium, transforms grief into agency and creates spaces of recognition, belonging, and hope.

2. UNDERSTANDING GENDER-BASED VIOLENCE IN SPAIN

This section examines the historical, academic and institutional evolution of Spain's response to gender-based violence. It traces how feminist activism, scholarship and state initiatives have progressively shaped public awareness, data collection and legal frameworks since the democratic transition. Beginning with the emergence of feminist analyses and early efforts to document violence, the section explores how these initiatives intersected with changing media discourses, the consolidation of equality policies and the development of landmark legislation such as the 2004 Organic Law on LOMPIVG. It also considers recent challenges, including the rise of far-right antifeminist narratives, which have sought to undermine advances achieved over the past three decades.

2.1 Data and Academic Approaches

Over the last 30 years, Spain has made significant progress in the study and response to gender-based violence. Academic research has evolved alongside advances in political, social and cultural equality. The case of Ana Orantes in 1997 represented a pivotal turning point: following her murder, scholarly work, national data collection efforts and surveys addressing gender violence increased significantly.

Before 1997, the feminist publication *Vindicación Feminista* served as a key platform where activists and writers publicly denounced violence against women and the aggressive attitudes they themselves experienced. The work of lawyer and writer Lidia Falcón is fundamental to understanding violence against women during a time when institutional interest and data collection were severely limited. In her book *Violencia contra la mujer* (1991), Falcón draws attention to the slow legal response to cases of violence and the lack of visibility caused by the impunity of perpetrators, sustained by a judicial system and a society unwilling to recognise women as victims rather than as complicit participants.

Several studies have further highlighted the collusion between the patriarchal system and violence against women (Amorós, 1990; Bosch et al., 2006, 1999; Maquieira & Sánchez, 1990). The issue has also been explored through analyses of media coverage of gender-based violence and femicides (Fagoaga, 1994; López Díez, 2003; Menéndez Menéndez, 2010, 2016). From the perspective of health sciences, scholars have examined the long-term consequences of violence on women, including suicide (Lorente Acosta et al., 2005).

Spain has also led pioneering research into the financial and societal costs of gender-based violence, including the burden on healthcare systems, judicial processes and support services, underscoring its wider societal impact. Public policies and legal strategies aimed at eradicating gender violence have been the focus of extensive research (Bodelón, 2014).

Since 1999, the Macro-surveys on Violence Against Women conducted by the Ministry of Equality have provided detailed data on the prevalence of physical, psychological and sexual violence among women aged 16–74. The 2019 edition revealed that 57.3% of women had experienced some form of violence in their lifetime. As of January 2003, the Government Delegation against Gender-Based Violence (Delegación del Gobierno contra la Violencia de Género), the official body responsible for collecting femicide data, has recorded 1,288 gender-based killings of women up to November 2024. In 2013, Spain began systematically collecting data on children murdered in the context of gender-based violence, reporting 24 cases of minors killed between 2013 and 2017 (Pastor-Gosálbez et al., 2021). Since 2006, the Observatory on Violence Against Women has published annual reports analysing patterns, statistical trends and assessments of public policies addressing gender-based violence (Ministerio de Igualdad, 2024).

2.2 Naming the Violence: Feminist Resistance and the Discursive Turn in Post-franco Spain

Violence against women has always existed in Spain, but it was during the country's transition to democracy (1975–1986) that feminist associations began to bring visibility to this and other issues affecting women. Spain had been under a dictatorship with explicitly antifeminist policies, in which the state and the Catholic Church enforced the ideal of female abnegation and submission. During the transition period, the feminist movement launched various campaigns and organised street demonstrations in major cities like Madrid and Barcelona. These protests contributed to greater public awareness of problems such as violence against women and the imprisonment of women for actions that were then criminalised under patriarchal legal and moral codes.

As Larumbe Gorraiz explains, 'the voice of feminism echoed through the streets, demanding legal equality, and a new social perception of women began to emerge in contrast to the dominant sexist stereotypes' (2004, p. 107). However, a profound transformation of social, political and economic structures was still needed to dismantle the discrimination faced by women.

There was an urgent need to challenge the cultural norms that viewed sexual assault as 'crimes against honour' (*delitos contra la honestidad*, as classified in Spain's penal code until 1989) and physical violence as legitimate punishment for disobedience, adultery or other supposed offences against a husband's or father's honour and reputation.

The creation of the Instituto de la Mujer (Women's Institute) in 1983 by the Spanish Socialist Workers' Party (PSOE) – which included several prominent feminist activists – marked the institutionalisation of feminism within the Spanish state. This development, alongside the grassroots efforts of feminist movements, played an important role in raising public awareness and putting gender-based violence on the political agenda (Valiente Fernández, 2006). While feminist activists denounced violence against women through protests and publications, Concha Fagoaga (1999) observes that at the time, feminist discourse on domestic violence remained largely absent or obscured in mainstream media. This was partly because the violence stemmed from gender relations embedded in a patriarchal system that was not recognised within institutional discourse and thus remained invisible in public narratives. Media reports on domestic abuse and femicides often framed such cases as isolated incidents or as the result of individual pathology, relying on stereotypes that concealed the structural nature of the violence. Common tropes included 'crimes of passion,' temporary insanity or the perpetrator's intoxication.

This 'rhetoric of concealment' dominated the media's portrayal of gender violence until the late 1990s. When Ana Orantes was murdered by her ex-husband in 1997, then–Deputy Prime Minister Francisco Álvarez-Cascos referred to her case as simply one of many 'isolated incidents' (El País, 1997). Such framing, as philosopher Celia Amorós later argued, prevented these cases from being counted and conceptualised as a specific form of systemic violence. It was only after Orantes's death that the concept of gender-based violence – coined by feminist movements – began to enter public discourse and catalyse political debate.

2.3 Legal Advances and Public Policies: From Silence to Protection

Categorising these cases as 'isolated' or 'crimes of passion' resulted in their exclusion from official counts and the conceptualisation of them as examples 'of a specific type of violence with a structural character,' as Amorós (2006) points out. The case of Ana Orantes was decisive in standardising and counting cases of violence against women, thereby incorporating the concept of gender-based violence – coined by feminists – into the public vocabulary, turning it into a topic of debate. Conceptualising abuse and femicides was enormously difficult according to Amorós (2006), but moving from anecdote to category politicised the problem and created demands for political measures to tackle the social issue of violence against women.

In Spain, the development of legislation has been key to establishing a comprehensive protection framework addressing the problem from legal, social, educational and preventive perspectives. The following examines the main laws and reforms implemented in Spain, analysing their impact in the fight against gender-based violence. The approval of Organic Law 1/2004 on LOMPIVG on 28 December marked an unprecedented advance by recognising gender violence as violence exercised against women for being women (BOE, 2004). At the time, it was one of the most progressive laws in Europe, pioneering a comprehensive approach that included prevention through equality education, social awareness, specialised courts and protection measures. This law laid important groundwork for Spain's later ratification of the Council of Europe's Istanbul Convention in 2014, further reinforcing its commitment to combating gender-based violence.

Regarding legal protection, the law established the creation of Specialised Courts for Violence against Women (Gender Violence Courts) and recognised free legal assistance for victims. The first courts were created in 2005, and as of 31 December 2022, there were 461 courts nationwide attending to gender violence cases. Of these, 113 are exclusive Gender Violence Courts and 348 are compatible courts. This law also includes protection and assistance measures such as shelters for women victims of gender-based violence and psychological support services (Pastor-Gosálbez et al., 2021, p. 111). In Spain, there are around 90 shelters distributed across the various autonomous communities. These provide a safe place for women and their children, offering psychological, legal and social support; notably, women do not have to file a complaint to access these shelters (p. 111). The law also established the need for training programmes for professionals in the judicial, healthcare and educational sectors. Thanks to this law, Spain was recognised by the European Agency for Fundamental Rights as a leading country in the fight against gender-based violence within the European Union (p. 111).

Other reforms reflect the need to adapt the legal framework to evolving patterns of violence and to guarantee greater protection for victims. Successive reforms of the Criminal Code in 2010 and 2015 strengthened the response to gender violence by incorporating stalking and digital violence, addressing new forms of aggression facilitated by technology. The increase of penalties for repeat offenders and aggravation of sentences in cases of especially cruel violence were also included in these reforms (BOE, 2010; 2015a). With the approval of Organic Law 8/2015 and Law 26/2015 on the Protection of Children and Adolescents Exposed to Gender-Based Violence, the protection system recognised minors exposed to gender violence as direct victims (BOE, 2015b; 2015c). This extension of the victim concept emphasises the importance of protecting children from the devastating effects of violence. Recent statistics show that from 2013 to early 2024, 60 minors have died in cases of gender violence against their mothers in Spain, and 438 minors have become orphans due to this violence (Delegación del Gobierno contra la Violencia de Género, 2024).

In 2017, the State Pact against Gender Violence was approved, representing an unprecedented political and social agreement in Spain (BOE, 2017). This law expanded the definition of gender violence beyond intimate partner relationships to include sexual, economic and vicarious violence. It also adopted specific measures to address violence in particularly vulnerable groups such as migrant women, older women and women with disabilities (BOE, 2017). The most recent legislation is the Comprehensive Guarantee of Sexual Freedom Law (known as the 'Only Yes Means Yes Law'), passed in 2022 (BOE, 2022). This law arose following the gang rape case of a young woman during the 2016 San Fermín festival that shocked Spanish society. It redefines sexual crimes, eliminating the distinction between abuse and assault, and places consent as the central axis (BOE, 2022).

2.4 Challenges and Counterforces: Feminist Critiques and the Far-Right Backlash in Spain

Despite the progress made, significant challenges remain. Resources and means provided by the administration have been insufficient, thereby preventing the full and effective implementation of the law. Other authors highlight the lack of social measures such as support programmes and the underdevelopment of prevention actions through education, healthcare and other professional sectors, which may contribute to the persistence of sexist and discriminatory biases in judicial processes and sentences (Pastor-Gosálbez et al., 2021, p. 118).

Moreover, feminist organisations that act as observatories of violence, such as Feminicidio.net, demand that femicide be legally recognised. The femicide data they provide exceed official figures, as they include murders of women outside intimate partner relationships and identify types not considered in official statistics, such as murders related to prostitution, among others (Informe España, 2023, p. 69). Feminicidio.net's 2023 Spain report documents 103 cases of women murdered that year, marking an increase compared to previous years. The report and other publications also warn about gender violence among younger populations, and the denial or trivialisation of violence observed among adolescent boys (Boneta et al., 2024). This reveals significant failures regarding violence prevention towards women and the consequences of abandoning co-education for equality (Informe España, 2023, pp. 77–78).

Despite legislative advances in Spain, cases of violence and femicides continue to rise, underscoring the need to promote a profound cultural shift that eradicates the roots of violence and fosters relationships based on equality and mutual respect. While the feminist movement has achieved great success as a social movement over recent decades, we are witnessing a patriarchal backlash rooted in a European political movement defined by antifeminism, which brings together far-right parties, headed in Spain by the ultra-right Vox party, which was supported by over three million voters in the 2019 general elections (Forti, 2021, p. 12).

This party employs 'post-truth,' combining half-truths or lies with an emotive tone to address controversial issues and make its discourse appear unquestionable (Álvarez-Benavides & Jiménez-Aguilar, 2020, p. 179). Vox has made gender violence a central axis of its anti-gender discourse in Spain. Although the 2004 Integral Law Against Gender Violence was approved unanimously and considered pioneering internationally, ultra-conservative sectors unsuccessfully attempted to challenge it. In 2014, Spain ratified the Istanbul Convention without controversy, consolidating its commitment to fighting gender violence. However, with Vox's arrival, political consensus on these policies has fractured, generating a new ideological dispute whose consequences remain to be seen (Cabezas Fernández, 2023, pp. 201–202).

Furthermore, this antifeminist backlash extends beyond the political arena, permeating social media and digital platforms, where messages reinforcing sexist stereotypes, trivialising gender-based violence and attempting to discredit activists and feminist movements are disseminated (Cappelle, 2023). This trend is part of a global surge in far-right populist discourses that instrumentalise antifeminism to mobilise conservative sectors and resist social changes propelled by feminist movements. Such political and social shifts present significant challenges for feminist movements, which must persist in their educational and political advocacy while also combating hate narratives and misinformation aimed at reversing the progress made in gender equality both in Spain and worldwide.

These ongoing social, legal and political transformations have also reverberated through Spain's cultural sphere, where music has become a powerful medium for articulating feminist resistance. Building on this cultural context, the next section turns to academic research, examining how scholars have theorised and analysed the intersections between music, feminism and gender-based violence in Spain.

3. VOICING RESISTANCE: FEMINIST READINGS OF MUSIC, GENDER-BASED VIOLENCE AND FEMICIDES IN SPAIN

Although Spain's vibrant feminist movements and the growing presence of gender-based violence narratives in popular music have transformed the cultural landscape, academic research on this intersection remains limited and fragmented. This section maps the main contributions to date, tracing how scholarly attention has gradually shifted from the analysis of sexist representations to the exploration of feminist musical responses. Such limited engagement reflects broader gaps in the theorisation and documentation of feminist cultural practices, where music has often been overlooked as a site of resistance, memory and social critique. It also reviews key empirical studies that document the increasing visibility of gender violence themes in Spanish popular music since the early 2000s.

3.1 Mapping the Field: From Absence to Visibility

Although music has long served as a vehicle for political dissent and cultural identity in Spain, academic research on its role in representing and challenging gender-based violence remains limited. Some studies have examined gender inequality in the music industry or analysed sexist messages in lyrics; however, few have directly addressed how Spanish music reflects, normalises or confronts violence against women, particularly femicide. This gap highlights the need for interdisciplinary approaches that bridge musicology, feminist theory and sociology. Since the 1980s, certain Spanish artists have addressed violence against women in their songs, but from the turn of the century, this theme progressively became a consistent element in popular musical discourse. Gómez Escarda et al. (2019) analysed a sample of 210 songs spanning four decades and found that, as social awareness of gender-based violence grew, popular music increasingly incorporated these themes. Traditionally dominant styles such as pop showed the highest representation, particularly during the periods 2000–2009 and 2010–2017, coinciding with the expansion of the feminist movement. Subsequent studies confirm that, from 2000 onwards, approximately 89 % of songs reflecting the full cycle of violence appear in this period. These songs span diverse genres, including pop, heavy metal, hip-hop/rap and rock, with pop achieving the greatest visibility among mass audiences (Hormigos-Ruiz et al., 2018).

3.2 Feminist Musical Activism and Collective Repertoires

Building on this overview, the following section examines how recent research has approached feminist musical activism through new interdisciplinary and technological methods. It highlights how the combination of quantitative and qualitative tools allows for a more nuanced understanding of sexism in music and situates Spanish studies within a broader, data-driven feminist scholarship. A recent study by Casanovas-Buliart et al. (2024), entitled *Evolution over 62 Years: An Analysis of Sexism in the Lyrics of the Most-Listened-to Songs in Spain*, offers an innovative approach to analysing sexism in Spanish popular music over more than six decades. Combining manual labelling techniques through crowdsourcing with machine learning tools, the research team analysed over 2,000 songs selected between 1960 and 2022, including historical chart-toppers and data extracted from the Spotify API. The lyrics were classified according to 10 distinct categories of sexist discourse, such as objectification, hypersexualisation, possessive control, gender stereotypes and rejection of feminism. This system enabled the training of an automated text classification model with high accuracy, applicable to large volumes of lyrics. The corpus included songs in Spanish (54%) and English (45%), with a small proportion (1.5%) in other languages. Notably, among the songs classified as sexist, 60 % were in Spanish, compared with 38 % in English, suggesting a higher density of sexist content in Spanish-language lyrics within the contemporary Spanish music market. This distribution highlights the centrality of Spanish in local music consumption while also emphasising the strong presence of Anglo-American music and the processes of linguistic hybridity characteristic of cultural globalisation. The study reveals that approximately 51% of the songs analysed contain sexist expressions, with a marked increase in the last two decades, coinciding with the consolidation of streaming as the dominant form of music consumption. Songs from genres such as Latin urban and Anglo-American pop stand out for their higher concentration of sexist messages, raising questions about the amplifying role of digital platforms in the reproduction of gender inequalities. Beyond its empirical value, this research study represents a methodological advance in the critical analysis of popular culture by articulating quantitative and qualitative approaches through a feminist perspective. Its findings confirm that symbolic violence against women found in music is not an isolated phenomenon but rather structural and evolving, and they reinforce the need to incorporate technological tools into the study of contemporary cultural representations.

3.3 From Representation to Resonance: Feminist Soundscapes and Urban Resistance

Arévalo et al. (2018) have documented how the representation of violence in Latin music has undergone a substantial shift: from explicit physical violence towards more subtle and symbolic forms, linked to control, objectification or the rejection of female autonomy. Although their study is not confined exclusively to Spain, it is highly relevant when considering the influence of global Latin music – particularly reggaetón and Latin trap – on Spanish audiences through streaming platforms. In the new millennium, music in Spain is situated within a transnational ecosystem where narratives of violence and sexism are produced, circulated and reconfigured in constant dialogue between the local and the global. In this shifting landscape, feminist anthems emerge as counterpoints, offering audiences songs that challenge sexist norms and resonate as tools of collective resistance.

In the recent academic landscape on urban music, the article by Espinal Ramírez et al. (2024) offers a systematic analysis of research trends surrounding reggaetón, reviewing 69 articles published between 2006 and 2022. The authors identify a predominance of women researchers (71% of the output), which, in their view, has contributed to introducing gender perspectives and critical approaches to sex-gender representations in this musical genre. The study reveals that much of the literature adopts a historical approach, addressing the origins and evolution of reggaetón, as well as its consolidation as a global sociocultural phenomenon. Within this framework, the reviewed works present divergent discourses. Some emphasise the role of reggaetón in reproducing stereotypes and violence against women. Others, however, highlight its potential as a space of subversion and empowerment. This is particularly evident in practices such as *perreo* – a reggaetón dance traditionally associated with hypersexualisation, now being re-signified in feminist contexts. Beyond mapping existing research, the article points to gaps that are particularly relevant for studying music in the new millennium and its relation to gender-based violence. Among these gaps, the lack of research on audiences, the identity construction that emerges from interaction with reggaetón and how these processes unfold in specific national contexts, including Spain, are particularly notable. The authors also emphasise the need to promote academic production from Latin America and in Spanish so that local cultural realities are represented rather than subsumed into Anglo-centric narratives. The evidence suggests that the influence of reggaetón and other urban music on social perceptions of gender-based violence is best understood within the transnational dynamics that shape and challenge contemporary Spanish cultural life. It also highlights how these musical forms are being re-signified by feminist movements in Spain, generating new modes of resistance and opportunities for identity construction.

In re-signifying genres such as reggaetón and transforming listening into participation, feminist musicians and audiences in Spain produce a shared sonic memory of resistance. This convergence between sound, affect and activism opens a historical trajectory that can be traced back to the feminist voices and musical practices emerging in the late Francoist period.

4. THE GENEALOGY OF FEMINIST SOUND IN SPAIN (1970S–1990S)

Building on the previous review of feminist musical research, this section traces the evolution of Spain's musical responses to gender-based violence and femicides from the late Francoist period to the present. It explores how songs have acted as mnemonic and affective sites where women's experiences of violence are voiced, remembered and politicised. Across different genres and historical moments – from early ballads and pop performances to reggaetón and protest anthems – music has provided an alternative archive of feminist resistance, challenging silences in the legal, media and institutional spheres.

While many of these songs respond to acts of violence, their message extends beyond individual tragedies. They expose feminicide as part of a broader continuum of coercion, control and everyday misogyny. As Gómez Escarda et al. (2019) observe, only a small proportion of Spanish songs depict the woman's death directly, while most address earlier stages of abuse, transforming music into a space of social pedagogy and collective awareness. Over the past five decades, feminist musical expression in Spain has evolved alongside major social and political transformations – from the early voices of dissent under Francoism to the contemporary resurgence of feminist protest through the 8M movement. The following sections trace this genealogy through distinct yet interconnected moments, showing how music has moved from representation to activism, from individual testimony to collective memory.

4.1 Early Echoes of Gender Violence in Song

Music in Spain has been a key tool for expressing social, political and cultural discontent, particularly during periods marked by repression. In the 1960s and 1970s, protest songs emerged in response to the final years of the Franco dictatorship, denouncing censorship, political repression, social inequality and the lack of basic freedoms. As Esther Pérez Villalba (2007) notes, singer-songwriters and political songs operated as cultural pro-democratic agents. While female artists were present in the music scene at the time, songs explicitly addressing violence against women or broader issues of gender discrimination and empowerment remained scarce.

Some Spanish women artists began to challenge *machismo* through their music. One emblematic example is 'Yo no soy esa' ['I Am Not That Woman', 1971] by Mari Trini, whose style blended melodic song, singer-songwriter traditions, pop and folk with influences from French chanson. The track became a feminist anthem for female empowerment, rejecting traditional gender roles and affirming women's independence and freedom. According to music journalist Miguel Ángel Bargueño (2019), Trini's work resonated deeply with women, giving voice to both those who suffered and those who resisted submission. The song's legacy continues, and it was recently reinterpreted by Ona Mafalda, a Spanish singer, who, in an interview on *Los 40 Principales*, a popular Spanish radio programme, described her version as a modern and empowered feminist statement (Zavala, 2025).

Perhaps the most iconic and pioneering figure in denouncing machismo in Spanish music is María Jiménez. With her flamenco style and defiant attitude, she performed numerous songs criticising male dominance and celebrating female autonomy. Her most well-known track, 'Se acabó' ['It's Over', 1978], is a powerful declaration of liberation from an abusive relationship. Decades later, following the unsolicited kiss that Luis Rubiales, then president of the Royal Spanish Football Federation, gave player Jennifer Hermoso after the final of the 2023 FIFA Women's World Cup, the song resurfaced as a viral feminist anthem under the hashtag #SeAcabó. The phrase became a rallying cry on social media and in street demonstrations, transforming Jiménez's words into a symbol of collective resistance to machismo and gender violence in contemporary Spain. This resurgence demonstrates how feminist memory operates through popular culture, as a song once rooted in personal defiance has become a transgenerational medium of protest and solidarity. Early denunciations of machismo, however, were often perceived as isolated, private experiences, as Spanish society was still shaped by what Ruiz Castillo (2006, p. 56) describes as a deeply rooted 'Spanish mentality,' in which patriarchal legal principles were reinforced through emotional education passed down from parents to children, confining women to the private sphere.

4.2 Feminism Without Theory: Defiance Through Music and Style

The Movida Madrileña emerged during Spain's transition to democracy as a countercultural movement that embraced experimentation with identity and challenged social norms inherited from Francoist Spain. As Maite Usoz de la Fuente (2015) situates it, the movement reconfigured urban cultural identity through postmodern media circuits. Building on this framework, Jorge Pérez (2014) highlights 'queer traces' in the soundtrack of the Movida, showing how performance and subversive sound destabilised traditional gender norms. Women artists played a crucial role in reshaping cultural perceptions of femininity, producing provocative lyrics, rebellious stage presence and transgressive attitudes that functioned as forms of resistance against the dominant patriarchal order.

A striking example of women's cultural resistance during the Movida Madrileña is the band Las Vulpes and their 1983 song 'Me gusta ser una zorra' ['I like being a slut'], a reinterpretation of The Stooges' 'I Wanna Be Your Dog'. While the original song, performed by men, passed without censorship, the female version provoked immediate scandal, media outrage and even legal action, illustrating the gendered double standards of post-Franco Spain (El País, 1983). In a retrospective 2020 interview with El País, the song's author, María ('Mamen') emphasised that they had no conscious connection to feminism at the time and were simply expressing themselves through their music and performance. Over time, the song has been retrospectively celebrated as a feminist punk anthem precisely because it reclaims female sexual autonomy, subverts male-coded musical material, and exposes societal hypocrisies (Marcos, 2020). The broader cultural impact of Las Vulpes is reflected in the 2005 film *El Calentito*, directed by Chus Gutiérrez. Although fictionalised, the film draws directly on their experience to explore a group of young women negotiating visibility, gender norms and self-expression in the Movida. Viewed from the present, both the song and its cinematic echo highlight how women's creative practices can generate enduring forms of resistance, even in the absence of explicit feminist ideology.

Meanwhile, Alaska, initially with the bands Kaka de Luxe and later with Alaska y Dinarama, championed messages of self-affirmation, gender dissidence and personal freedom. Her 1986 track 'A quién le importa' ['Who Cares'] became widely recognised as an anthem for the LGBTQ+ community while also functioning as a feminist declaration of independence from normative social expectations. The song's lyrics and Alaska's public persona challenged conventional gender roles and heteronormative norms, exemplifying how women in the Movida used music and performance to assert autonomy and resist patriarchal pressures. As noted by Vegas in an article in *Vanity Fair* (2016), the song's enduring popularity and its adoption across various social contexts underscore its cultural significance.

Such practices exemplify what may be described as a form of feminism without theory through acts of cultural and bodily resistance that challenge patriarchal norms even when they are not articulated within formal academic or activist discourse. Women artists in the Movida embodied this form of feminism through everyday practices such as aesthetic defiance, the rejection of traditional gender roles and assertive public self-expression. Their performative agency transformed their bodies, voices and images from objects of male consumption into tools of resistance. As Judith Butler (1990) argues, gender is an ongoing performance, and the repeated subversion of normative acts can challenge existing power structures. Viewed through this lens, the provocative performances and public personas of Las Vulpes and Alaska exemplify a lived, performative feminism that, though not explicitly theorised at the time, disrupted patriarchal and heteronormative expectations and created new spaces for female agency, self-definition and cultural resistance. Their use of voice, sound and gesture thus made gender itself audible as performance, translating Butler's notion of performativity into a distinctly sonic and visual rebellion.

Despite the visibility and gender dissent that emerged during La Movida, violence against women remained conspicuously absent in the lyrics of popular Spanish music. Songs such as 'Bailando' ['Dancing'] by Alaska y Los Pegamoides or 'Perlas ensangrentadas' ['Bloodstained Pearls'] by Dinarama, while subversive in their aesthetics and attitudes, did not directly address gender-based violence. This omission persisted in much of the music of the era where machismo and misogyny were often normalised or romanticised. Los Ronaldos' 1987 track *'Sí, sí'* [*'Yes, yes'*] features a refrain that narrates escalating sexual aggression as if it were part of a flirtatious encounter. This portrayal, which culminates in an explicit reference to rape, generated significant public condemnation and prompted legal action. In 1988, feminist organisations in the Basque Country and Navarra filed a complaint arguing that the song openly encouraged sexual violence (Muez, 1988). Similarly, Loquillo y Trogloditas' 'La mataré' ['I Will Kill Her'] (1987) narrates the obsessive and violent thoughts of a man towards a woman. Despite its commercial success, the song faced criticism for glorifying gender-based violence though Loquillo defended it as a portrayal of a disturbed character rather than an endorsement of such behaviour. These songs reflect a tendency in the popular music of the time to trivialise or even glorify violence against women, without offering critical reflection on the issue.

4.3 Music as Activism Against Gender-Based Violence and Femicides

As the shadow of Ana Orantes loomed over Spanish public life, the music scene began to resonate with a newfound urgency. Yet, throughout much of the 1990s, direct references to gender-based violence remained rare. Instead, a handful of female singer-songwriters turned inward, crafting what one might call a poetics of discomfort, with intimate critiques of emotional oppression, romantic entrapment and the symbolic misuse of love. It was only as the turn of the century approached that Spanish popular music began to make explicit space for denunciation. According to the comparative study *Música y violencia de género en España* (Hormigos-Ruiz et al., 2018), nearly 89% of the 210 songs, spanning several decades, that fully depicted the 'cycle of violence' were released after the year 2000. The 1990s were therefore a quiet interim – a time of introspection rather than overt protest, where artists explored emotional structures that enabled violence but stopped short of naming it explicitly.

At the end of the 1990s and the beginning of the new millennium, music in Spain began to assume a more explicit role in denouncing gender-based violence. In this context, Cristina del Valle emerged as one of the most visible voices of feminist activism within the artistic sphere. Known for her career in the duo Amistades Peligrosas and her solo work, del Valle combined her musical endeavours with a consistent social commitment, denouncing femicides and sexist aggression through both her artistic output and public engagement (Del Valle, 2025).

In 1999, she promoted the creation of the Plataforma de Mujeres Artistas contra la Violencia de Género, an initiative aimed at making male violence visible and pressuring for the enactment of comprehensive protective legislation.

This project brought together women artists from different musical and performing disciplines, united by the conviction that music could serve as a vehicle for social transformation. Among its most emblematic initiatives was the show *Ellas dan la nota*, first presented in 2002, which combined music, poetry and theatre to raise awareness of women's situations in Spain and other international contexts. The performance toured stages in Mexico, Palestine and Baghdad, becoming a reference point for music committed to gender justice. The activities and impact of the platform were documented in the book *Ellas dan la nota: la aventura de la Plataforma de Mujeres Artistas contra la Violencia de Género* (De Miguel, 2004), which provides a detailed account of the musical, theatrical and public initiatives aimed at raising awareness about gender-based violence in Spain and beyond. These performances exemplify what Elizabeth Jelin (2002) describes as *Los trabajos de la memoria* [*The Work of Memory*], collective acts that transform private suffering into public meaning. Through song and testimony, the Platform mobilised the memory of women's lived experiences of violence, transforming them into collective expressions of solidarity and political demand. For Jelin, memory work involves social actors who struggle to define and name what took place during periods of violence, as well as those who seek to honour and give public recognition to the victims. Through their performances, the artists of the Platform assumed precisely this role, transforming commemoration into activism.

Del Valle's activism was deeply personal. In an interview, she revealed that she was a victim of gender-based violence and had experienced abuse in her own home during her childhood. She stated, 'I am a child victim of violence in my home like thousands of women and also many of my fellow artists; it is a reality that crosses all social classes, ages, and cultures; it is called *machismo* and permeates all of society' (Europa Press, 2017). In her musical repertoire, del Valle addresses themes of gender-based violence directly. One notable example is her song 'Encadenada' ['Chained'], released in 1999 as part of her album *El Dios de las Pequeñas Cosas* (Del Valle, 1999), whose lyrics reflect personal and social dimensions of abuse and entrapment. Through these actions, Cristina del Valle exemplifies how artists of the transitional period into the new century used music as both an aesthetic expression and a political instrument to denounce gender-based violence and femicides.

The early 2000s marked a decisive shift in Spanish popular music's engagement with gender-based violence. Reincidentes' '¡Ay, Dolores!' (['Oh, Dolores!'], 2000, punk/rock) denounced domestic violence with unflinching clarity, narrating the pain and silencing of battered women, while Boikot's 'Bajo el suelo' (['Under the Ground'], 2000, ska-punk) voiced the visceral trauma of abuse from a female perspective. Female artists also began to assert their voices explicitly across diverse musical genres. Bebe (pop/rock, flamenco-influenced) emerged with her debut album *Pafuera Telarañas* (2004), which included 'Malo' ['Bad'], a direct critique of domestic abuse that became an anthem of empowerment and public awareness (Gómez Escarda et al., 2019). Pasión Vega (flamenco, copla) addressed female suffering and resilience in her repertoire, blending traditional styles with social critique. La Oreja de Van Gogh (pop-rock) contributed with 'No vales más que yo' ['You are not Worthier Than Me'] (2003), which highlighted psychological control and emotional abuse in intimate relationships. Amaral (pop-rock/folk) produced emotionally charged songs such as 'Salir corriendo' ['Running Away'] (2002), reflecting relational toxicity and emotional entrapment, though not explicitly addressing physical violence or femicide. Finally, Mala Rodríguez (hip-hop/rap) brought a confrontational urban perspective with lyrics that reflected women's anger, resistance and critique of patriarchal oppression in tracks such as 'Quién Manda' ['Who's in Charge'] (2003), merging social denunciation with feminist empowerment, as she recounts in her book *Cómo ser Mala* (Rodríguez, 2021). Together, these artists exemplify a moment in which Spanish music as a platform for social consciousness, public shock and activism against gender-based violence and femicides, across a variety of musical languages and audiences.

5. AFFECTIVE POLITICS AND COLLECTIVE SOUNDSCAPES (2000S–2010S)

Following the historical trajectory outlined in the previous section, this part turns to the 21st century to explore how feminist music in Spain expands from representation to affective mobilisation. It examines how emotions, memory and collective soundscapes have become key forces in feminist activism, transforming protest into a shared politics of feeling and listening.

5.1 Feminist Anthems and Affective Resistance Against Violence and Femicides

Since the early 2010s, the feminist movement in Spain has undergone an unprecedented expansion, positioning itself at the centre of public debate and the political agenda. A major turning point came on 8 March 2018, when the so-called feminist strike mobilised millions of women under the slogan 'If we stop, the world stops'. This was not a traditional labour strike but a multifaceted action in which women were called to stop working, refrain from attending classes, cease care work and reduce consumption (Campillo, 2019).

The 2018 8M strike in Spain was part of a broader wave of international feminist mobilisations. One year earlier, on 8 March 2017, an International Women's Strike had been called by the global feminist movement, following major mass mobilisations in countries such as Argentina, Poland, the USA and Spain (Watkins, 2018). More than 30 countries joined the call, including Spain, where the feminist movement organised, for the first time, a fourfold strike: a 24-hour halt of care work, education and consumption, alongside a (partial) labour strike (Watkins, 2018). This international framework provided both inspiration and strategic guidance for Spanish feminists, demonstrating how a multifaceted strike could highlight the invisible labour of women and challenge gendered inequalities. By adapting these global experiences to the Spanish context, the 8M strike was able to mobilise millions, occupy public spaces and create a visible, symbolic challenge to patriarchal structures (Campillo, 2019). The figures were striking, with an estimated 5.3 million women taking part in strikes and demonstrations across the country in 2018, and the 2019 mobilisation consolidating itself as one of the largest social movements in Spain's recent history (Idoiaga Mondragón et al., 2020). The scale of the protests was reflected not only in international media coverage but also in symbolic gestures of great resonance. Many women left their daily responsibilities in the hands of men to take to the streets, and even Queen Letizia cancelled her official engagements on that day (Campillo, 2019), underlining the transversal reach and political significance of the movement.

These mobilisations must also be read against a backdrop marked by widespread outrage over cases of sexual violence and femicide. In her essay 'Affective Economies' (2004), Sara Ahmed explains how emotions circulate between bodies and align individuals with communities through shared attachments and intensities. Emotions, she argues, do things as they move, bind and create the very surfaces and boundaries that allow the individual and the collective to emerge (Ahmed, 2004, p. 119). This framework helps illuminate how anger, fear and grief became the affective glue of Spain's contemporary feminist movement, transforming personal trauma into collective energy and mobilising political action.

The most emblematic example of this affective transformation was the case of La Manada (2016–2018), in which the gang rape of a young woman during the San Fermín festival and the subsequent court ruling triggered an unprecedented wave of protests. The public response, particularly among young women, turned the slogan 'It's not abuse, it's rape' into a collective outcry that filled streets and squares. The La Manada case acted as a catalyst for a broader feminist consciousness, linking outrage over sexual violence with structural demands for equality and justice. The sustained and widespread protests, including the 8M strikes and other internationally inspired actions, created the social and political pressure that ultimately contributed to the approval of Spain's 'Solo sí es sí' law, which redefined consent and strengthened protections against sexual assault (Faraldo-Cabana, 2021; Navarro & Coromina, 2020).

The feminist strikes and demonstrations of 8M thus became one of the most powerful embodiments of collective resistance in contemporary Spain. Each year, thousands of women take to the streets, transforming public space into a resonant field of protest where music, chanting and rhythm articulate demands for equality and justice. The chants and songs of the 8M marches materialise these affective economies, turning anger and grief into shared political energy and transforming emotion itself into a mode of feminist resistance.

5.2 Singing the Strike: Memory, Protest and the Sound of 8M

These affective economies found one of their most audible expressions in the chants and songs of the 8M demonstrations, where collective sound became both the medium and the embodiment of feminist solidarity. Music played a crucial role in these mobilisations, as chants and songs functioned not only as tools of protest but also as collective rituals of empowerment. The use of sounds such as *cacerolazos* (banging of pots and pans), vocal chants and adapted songs like 'A la huelga' ['To the Strike'] transformed the streets into spaces of sonic resistance, making feminist demands audible and visible while fostering an atmosphere of unity and collective strength.

As Rigney (2018) argues, cultural memory should not be understood as a static repository of the past but as a dynamic practice continually reactivated through performance, circulation and affective engagement. Through what she terms 'remembering hope', Rigney shifts attention from the commemoration of trauma to the mobilisation of memory as a resource for collective agency and future-oriented activism. This approach resonates with Diana Taylor's (2003) notion of the repertoire as an embodied archive that transmits social knowledge and memory through live, ephemeral acts of performance. As Taylor explains, 'performances function as vital acts of transfer, transmitting social knowledge, memory, and a sense of identity through reiterated behaviour' (p. 2). The repertoire, encompassing gestures, movement, orality, dance and song, 'enacts embodied memory' and 'keeps and transforms choreographies of meaning' (pp. 20–21). Together, these frameworks illuminate how collective singing during the feminist strike transformed remembrance into a performative act of resonance and renewal.

The feminist re-singing of 'A la huelga' exemplifies this living process of memory transmission: the recovery of a historical archive and its transformation into a performative act of resonance and renewal. The song was originally composed by Chicho Sánchez Ferlosio in 1963 as part of his album *Canciones de la resistencia española* [Songs of the Spanish Resistance]. It became an anthem of anti-Francoist struggle, representing opposition to dictatorship and social repression. In the context of the 2018 feminist mobilisations, the song was adapted by feminist collectives such as Feministes Indignades, who modified the lyrics to reflect contemporary women's demands. The adapted version, titled '¡A la huelga, compañera!' ['To the Strike, Sister!'], became a powerful symbol during the 8M demonstrations, especially in cities like Bilbao, where thousands of women sang it in unison (El Confidencial, 2018). The new lyrics addressed issues such as labour inequality, the burden of unpaid domestic work and gender-based violence, establishing a bridge between past and present struggles. This act of reclaiming historical memory honours previous generations while strengthening the collective identity of the contemporary feminist movement.

The original version of '*A la huelga*' emphasised the collective mobilisation of working-class communities, evoking images of labourers leaving their workplaces and coming together in a unified call for a general strike. Its focus lay in portraying class solidarity as a force capable of confronting structural oppression.

In contrast, the feminist adaptation reframed the song through the lens of contemporary gender politics. The revised lyrics urged women to withdraw their labour from both paid employment and the domestic sphere, explicitly naming the everyday tools and technologies associated with feminised work. The new version also highlighted issues such as precarious contracts, lack of social protection and the unequal distribution of household responsibilities, exposing how economic and reproductive labour are systematically devalued. Through these changes, feminist collectives transformed the song into an anthem that linked historical class struggles with the present-day fight against gendered exploitation and inequality.

This adaptation retains the structure and rhythm of the original while re-orienting its message towards contemporary feminist struggles, bridging historical memory and current activism within a shared performative space of resistance. As Rigney (2018) observes, the memory–activism nexus operates through a dynamic exchange between remembering past struggles and shaping future ones. The feminist re-singing of 'A la huelga' thus exemplifies what she terms civic memory – a vortex of recollection and political action in which inherited repertoires of protest are reactivated as tools of contemporary mobilisation.

In reclaiming and transforming 'A la huelga', feminist collectives revived a song of labour struggle and redefined its emotional and political resonance. The collective act of singing together performs a bodily politics of memory, re-inscribing past voices into the present through rhythm and repetition. This same affective logic underpins later feminist anthems of healing, such as 'La Puerta Violeta'.

5.3 Voices of Healing: From 'La Puerta Violeta' to New Feminist Anthems

If in Section 4.4 the notion of affective economies proposed by Sara Ahmed (2004) helped illuminate the collective emotions mobilised during the 8M demonstrations, in this section attention shifts to a different aspect of her work. In *The Promise of Happiness* (2010), Ahmed explores how the pursuit of happiness and well-being operates as a technology of governance that regulates which emotions are deemed acceptable and whose pain must remain invisible. Within this framework, feminist and queer subjects appear as 'unhappy figures' who disturb normative happiness narratives and expose the violence concealed within them. As Ahmed (2010, p. 66) explains, feminist subjects are often represented as 'killjoys' whose refusal to smile or comply with happiness norms exposes how such narratives conceal forms of structural violence. Yet, it is precisely through this discomfort that alternative affective modes of resilience and repair emerge. These affective archives of unhappiness, as Ahmed calls them (2010, p. 18), make visible the pain that happiness narratives seek to erase.

Rozalén's 'La Puerta Violeta' can be read in this light as a feminist articulation of emotional reparation, where music transforms pain and vulnerability into the promise of healing and collective affirmation. By stepping through the purple door, the protagonist reorients herself away from the normative objects of happiness – home, submission, romantic love – towards collective freedom and affective autonomy. In this sense, the song enacts what Ahmed calls 'the freedom to be unhappy', transforming unhappiness into a condition of political insight and collective transformation (p. 195). Released in 2017, 'La Puerta Violeta' quickly became one of the most emblematic feminist anthems in contemporary Spanish popular music. The song emerged amid growing public awareness of gender-based violence and has since been adopted by feminist movements as a symbol of resilience and collective hope. Built around the image of a purple door – the colour historically associated with feminist struggle – the lyrics chart a movement from entrapment and silence to liberation and self-recognition.

The opening section situates the listener in a domestic environment shaped by fear and emotional withdrawal. The song introduces a young girl who appears hesitant to speak, reflecting the silencing effects of abuse. The figure of a disruptive and aggressive presence within the home functions both as an allusion to the perpetrator of violence and as a metaphor for the psychological turmoil that violence produces, conveying a sense of danger that permeates everyday life. As the narrative develops, the protagonist imagines a route towards liberation through the recurring image of the purple door. She describes stepping outside while allowing herself to cry openly, reclaiming her voice as a source of strength and using affective expression as a means of healing. The movement from interior confinement to public space becomes a symbolic passage from vulnerability to empowerment, underscoring the transformative potential of collective and expressive agency.

Healing through voice becomes the song's emotional core. Singing is transformed into an act of self-repair that reclaims agency through sound and embodiment. The melody mirrors this trajectory as it begins in a minor key – intimate and introspective – and gradually expands towards a brighter tonal register. Percussion and choral backing introduce a sense of elevation and collective force. The musical structure thus mirrors the lyrical passage from isolation to shared affirmation, suggesting that recovery is both an individual and a collective process sustained through emotional resonance.

The affective power of 'La Puerta Violeta' expanded beyond its original release when it became collectively reappropriated during the 8M marches. Sung in unison by thousands of women, the song's personal narrative of healing was transformed into a public act of solidarity. The singular *yo* (I) of the lyrics turned into a collective *nosotras* (we, female), and the act of singing together performed the very reorientation that Ahmed describes: a movement away from prescribed forms of happiness towards shared affective freedom. Each repetition of the chorus became an embodied assertion of survival and belonging, making 'La Puerta Violeta' a song of personal recovery and a living archive of feminist resistance and care.

6. CONTEMPORARY RECONFIGURATIONS: DIGITAL FEMINISM AND URBAN SOUND

This final section examines how contemporary Spanish feminist movements have reconfigured the relationship between sound, body and collective resistance. From the hypersexualised aesthetics of reggaetón to the viral resonance of *#SeAcabó*, music and digital media have become key arenas where gendered power relations are both reproduced and contested. These cultural practices reveal how popular music functions as entertainment and as a terrain of affective politics – where memory, emotion and embodiment articulate forms of feminist justice 'from below' (Segato, 2013). The analysis traces two interconnected processes: first, the feminist re-appropriation of reggaetón through *perreo combativo* and embodied pleasure and second, the transformation of María Jiménez's 'Se acabó' into a twenty-first-century rallying cry, reactivated by the digital mobilisation of #SeAcabó. Together, they illustrate how Spain's feminist soundscape moves between street, stage and screen, turning rhythm and voice into instruments of collective remembrance and resistance.

6.1 Patriarchal Rhythms: From Machismo to Resistance

This section examines how reggaetón, a genre born within the patriarchal structures of urban marginality, has evolved from reproducing machismo and female objectification to becoming a site of feminist reappropriation and embodied resistance. By tracing its trajectory from Puerto Rico's underground scene to its feminist reinvention in Spain, the analysis reveals how rhythm, language and performance operate as contested terrains where gendered power is both inscribed and subverted.

6.1.1. Reggaetón's Origins and Gendered Power

Reggaetón emerged in Puerto Rico in the early 1990s as part of the so-call 'underground' scene, rooted in the informal production and distribution of rap and reggae by youth from working-class neighbourhoods, *caseríos* and *barrios* (Rivera, 2009a, 2009b). Circulating through small-scale networks rather than mainstream media, the music combined US rap, Jamaican dancehall and Caribbean rhythms, expressing urban realities and Afro-Caribbean traditions. This underground scene offered young people a space for identity and resistance outside institutional control. Its growing visibility in 1994–1995 provoked moral panic among authorities, educators and media, leading to police raids and the confiscation of recordings (Rivera, 2009a, 2009b). State authorities and conservative groups framed the genre as obscene and dangerous, targeting marginalised youth whose bodies were portrayed as vulnerable to its influence. Yet such repression also revealed reggaetón's role as a vehicle of expression and dissent (Rivera, 2009a, 2009b). Contemporary artists like Residente and Bad Bunny have since turned it into a medium for civic engagement and political critique (Laborde, 2019). At the same time, the genre's impact cannot be separated from its treatment of gender and sexuality. From its beginnings, reggaetón drew on street language that conveyed authenticity but also provoked criticism for its explicit depictions of sex, desire and power. This vernacular style, often celebrated as transgressive, frequently reproduced misogynistic discourses that portrayed women as passive objects or commodities within a patriarchal framework (Carballo Villagra, 2006). The tension between reggaetón's visibility for marginalised youth and its reinforcement of gendered inequality lies at the heart of ongoing debates about the genre.

The expansion of reggaetón in Spain in the early 2000s unfolded through two parallel processes: its commercial assimilation by the music industry and its appropriation by Latin American migrant communities. The industry packaged it as a disposable, exoticised product, erasing its Caribbean roots through 'tropicalisation'. Meanwhile, migrant communities built their own networks – clubs, radio stations and local labels – where reggaetón became a marker of identity and a way to re-signify migration. This dual expansion created a 'double life' for the genre in Spain: a commercial trend and a vehicle of belonging (Arias Salvado, 2021). In Spain, debates on gender soon became central to its reception. Carballo Villagra (2006) identifies three dominant masculine archetypes in the genre: the macho, defined by sexual potency; the violent man, whose virility rests on aggression; and the successful man, legitimised by luxury and wealth. Within this framework, women appear as the 'other': fragmented, silenced and objectified. Carballo concludes that rather than censorship, the challenge lies in recognising reggaetón's role in shaping gender relations and promoting more egalitarian interactions between men and women.

6.1.2. Reclaiming the Beat: Feminist Perreo *and the Politics of the Body*

Despite differences in methodology and focus, recent studies on reggaetón converge on several key points regarding its reinforcement of patriarchal norms and gender-based violence. Scholars highlight the genre's hegemonic discourse, which consolidates stereotypes of masculinity rooted in machismo, sexual dominance and social power (Carballo Villagra, 2006; Bas-Peña & Pastor-Bravo, 2024; Espinal Ramírez et al., 2024). Women are often portrayed as sexual objects subordinated to male desire, described through animalising terms such as *gata* ('cat'), *perra* ('bitch'), or *fiera* ('beast'). This zoomorphic vocabulary functions as both verbal violence and objectification, even if some female artists later re-appropriate these labels to contest their meanings. In Spain, however, a new generation of women artists has reclaimed reggaetón's soundscape. Figures such as Brisa Fenoy, Tremenda Jauría and Ms Nina strategically appropriate the genre's musical and performative codes to subvert its patriarchal conventions (Araüna et al., 2020). This phenomenon – often called female perreo – marks a process of cultural and bodily re-appropriation, transforming a space historically tied to male control into one of female agency and resistance. Centring women's voices, desire and pleasure, these artists challenge the genre's *machista* foundations and re-signify its performative language as a tool for empowerment and critique.

Rita Laura Segato explains that patriarchal violence operates through the appropriation of women's bodies as territories of conquest, where masculine sovereignty inscribes itself through domination and control (2013, p. 17). Within the reggaetón imaginary, this logic of *dueñidad* – the presumption of male ownership over women's bodies – has historically been performed through both lyrical content and corporeal codes of dance. The woman's body is rendered visible only as the object of male desire, a landscape to be conquered, disciplined and displayed. Yet it is precisely within this space of hypervisibility that new feminist practices of perreo emerge. By re-appropriating the same rhythmic and choreographic language once used to objectify them, female artists and dancers transform perreo into a scene of resistance, where the body ceases to be the site of conquest and becomes instead a territory of autonomy and self-definition. In Segato's terms, this represents a shift from the logic of *dueñidad* to a 'justice from below' (p. 78), a collective reclamation of agency through embodied pleasure and affective solidarity. Through movement and rhythm, feminist perreo re-signifies the language of domination into a performative grammar of freedom, pleasure and repair. The emergence of these artists coincides with Spain's vibrant feminist movement, particularly the mass 8M demonstrations, where perreo functions simultaneously as an erotic dance and a political act of resistance – a site of collective empowerment and feminist expression. Their work aligns with what Damaly González (2023) terms *perreo combativo* ('combative twerking') and *neoperreo* ('new-style twerking'), movements emerging from transnational feminist, queer and trans collectives. For González, perreo in the digital era operates as both erotic and political practice – a collective act of resistance and self-empowerment that dismantles the patriarchal logic of desire. These strategies resonate strongly with Spanish artists who use the genre's performative power to reclaim pleasure and redefine public space as a site of feminist expression.

Songs such as Brisa Fenoy's 'Ella' ('She', 2018) and Ms Nina's 'Fresita' ('Little Strawberry,' 2017) exemplify this feminist transformation of reggaetón. In 'Ella', Fenoy articulates a celebration of women's autonomy by portraying a protagonist who claims ownership over her body and her happiness, rejecting the need for external approval. Although voiced in the third person, the song performs a collective assertion of women's right to self-determination and emotional fulfilment. Similarly, 'Fresita' reframes erotic expression as a site of empowerment rather than domination. Here, the singer emphasises her control over her body, her movements and her desire, transforming the aesthetics of *perreo* into an explicit declaration of agency. Through this repositioning, sensuality becomes a medium of power, not vulnerability, signalling a broader feminist reclamation of pleasure within contemporary urban music.

Together, these songs displace the genre's traditional logic of control, replacing submission and objectification with lyrical affirmation and bodily autonomy. These feminist practices and discourses offer not only symbolic resistance but also foster a critical culture that confronts machista violence. While femicide rarely appears explicitly in lyrics, denunciations of control, coercion and harassment provide the cultural backdrop that sustains feminist awareness. In this context, perreo combativo functions as both protest and pedagogy, exposing structural violence, transforming the dance floor into a site of collective visibility and turning pleasure itself into a mode of empowerment and resistance (Uribe-Molina, 2022).

6.2 'Se acabó': From Personal Liberation to Collective Outcry

As discussed earlier in Section 4.3, Elizabeth Jelin's (2002) concept of *los trabajos de la memoria* frames remembrance as a collective process that transforms private suffering into public meaning. Returning to Jelin's perspective here allows us to consider how memory also persists through cultural artefacts that move beyond direct testimony. Songs such as 'Se acabó' can thus be read as affective archives where the memory of gendered violence is stored, reactivated and transmitted through sound. For Jelin, memory work involves social actors who struggle to name and give meaning to experiences of violence. For Hirsch (2012, p. 5), postmemory describes how affect and imagination mediate the transmission of those experiences across generations. While Hirsch's model refers to inherited trauma, 'Se acabó' also speaks to the persistence of gendered violence in the present. It is not only a recollection of the past but an ongoing testimony of structural inequality that continues to shape women's lives. In this sense, 'Se acabó' occupies a space between postmemory and continuity as it draws on the affective archive of past trauma while transforming it into collective resistance. Through the voice and body of María Jiménez, the song reclaims the memory of violence as both inheritance and refusal – a sonic gesture that retrieves what has been silenced and turns it into affirmation. The song thus enacts what Jelin would call a 'social work of memory' through performance while reactivating the emotional repertoire of feminist remembrance in Spain's cultural soundscape.

6.2.1. Singing Defiance: Voice, Rhythm and Liberation in 'Se acabó'

Released in 1978, 'Se acabó' marked a radical moment in Spanish popular music and in the public articulation of female resistance. Written by Manuel Alejandro and performed by María Jiménez, the song blends *rumba flamenca* with pop-inflected instrumentation, combining the rhythmic pulse of *flamenco compás* with a danceable tempo that made its message accessible to mass audiences. Within a genre traditionally dominated by male narratives, Jiménez's interpretation subverts the conventions of the *flamenco-rumba* by introducing a distinctly feminist voice. The woman does not sing of loss but of rupture; not of submission but of survival transforming personal pain into audible defiance.

Musically, the song's structure and rhythm embody rupture. Each verse builds in intensity until the refrain, where the beat briefly halts in a percussive silence that precedes the emphatic '¡Se acabó!' ('It's over!'). This suspension becomes a sonic enactment of resistance, as the pause interrupts both the musical rhythm and the cycle of abuse. When the beat resumes, the listener perceives transformation and the re-emergence of a woman's voice that has regained control over tempo and tone. Jiménez's raspy timbre, at once wounded and defiant, heightens the emotional tension and turns the act of singing into an embodied gesture of liberation. The lyrics narrate the end of an abusive relationship in the first person, transforming domestic violence – a topic silenced in 1970s Spain – into audible protest.

The song opens with a forceful assertion of closure that frames leaving as both a bodily effort and an act of conscious will. The protagonist situates emancipation in her own decision-making, emphasising that freedom is something she chooses and enacts rather than something granted to her. The imagery of breaking through an emotional barrier conveys the dismantling of the patriarchal structures that once confined her, transforming endurance into a route towards self-determination.

As the narrative progresses, her stance becomes uncompromising. She expresses a desire to cut all ties with the abuser – visual, auditory, and emotional – using a sequence of refusals that produces a rhythmic pattern of negation. This accumulation turns absence into a deliberate tactic: withdrawing attention and emotion becomes a way of reclaiming power, allowing silence to function as a counter-violence that reorders the dynamics of control.

The following section intensifies this autonomy by rejecting the material comforts often used to sustain patriarchal dependency. She dismisses wealth, luxury and stability as irrelevant to her sense of worth, positioning personal freedom as the only meaningful resource. Her repeated assertion that fear no longer governs her life operates as a performative act: each reiteration diminishes the affective residue of abuse, transforming vulnerability into resonance. The song reaches its emotional peak when the musical progression momentarily halts, and she reiterates her declaration of finality with renewed force. This disruption of the cyclical rumba structure converts the song's rhythm from circularity to forward motion, signalling an irreversible transition towards liberation.

In her televised performances (RTVE Archivo, 1978), Jiménez reinforces this defiance visually. Dressed in bold, bright fabrics, she stands upright, her body still and commanding. There is no coquettish gesture, no ornamental movement; her power lies in stillness. Unlike the traditional female flamenco figure – often framed as the object of male spectatorship – Jiménez meets the camera's gaze head-on. She does not sing to a lover but to an audience that witnesses her refusal. The rumba rhythm – traditionally associated with festivity and sensuality – is recontextualised as a vehicle for feminist self-assertion, turning the end of abuse into the beginning of autonomy, an early act of speaking to power through music.

Through its fusion of lyrical agency, rhythmic interruption and vocal intensity, 'Se acabó' functions as both testimony and transformation: it translates trauma into rhythm, silence into beat and vulnerability into sound. In doing so, it inaugurates a genealogy of feminist musical expression in Spain where the act of singing 'it's over' becomes the first performative gesture of liberation. Listening to 'Se acabó' today, we hear not only one woman's defiance but the beginnings of a shared memory. Its rhythm – moving between momentum and stillness – echoes the cycles of pain and recovery that shape feminist experience.

6.2.2. Resurgence and #SeAcabó

Forty-five years after its release, 'Se acabó' resurfaced in 2023 as the anthem of a new wave of feminist uprising in Spain. What began in 1978 as the personal declaration of a woman breaking free from domestic abuse was reactivated through collective memory at a moment of national reckoning. In August 2023, following Spain's victory in the FIFA Women's World Cup, the non-consensual kiss that football federation president Luis Rubiales forced upon player Jennifer Hermoso provoked widespread outrage (Snape & Kassam, 2023). Within hours, the phrase 'Se acabó' flooded social media under the hashtag #SeAcabó, transforming a spontaneous expression of solidarity into a national statement: enough.

The hashtag functioned simultaneously as slogan, chant and echo of Jiménez's original cry. Activists, journalists and ordinary users adopted it to denounce everyday sexism, institutional complicity and the double standards that persist in Spanish public life. As *The Guardian* observed, #SeAcabó became 'Spain's Me Too moment', signalling a shift from isolated indignation to shared feminist consciousness (Ramírez, 2023). Unlike the global #MeToo movement, which began among high-profile women in the entertainment industry, #SeAcabó is rooted in the everyday and the communal. Its strength lies in its accessibility and its popular emotional charge. It brings together the football pitch, the domestic sphere, the workplace and the digital arena, connecting women from different social and generational backgrounds through a shared phrase and rhythm. In this new digital soundscape, the rhythm of Jiménez's refrain returned as a textual beat – short, percussive and collective. The temporal gap between 1978 and 2023 collapses into a single affective gesture, a transgenerational act of refusal that binds both moments together.

This resurgence reached its most eloquent visual and sonic articulation in the official campaign launched by the Ministry of Equality for the International Day for the Elimination of Violence against Women (25 November 2023). The short film, titled *Se acabó. Ahora ya España es otra* ['It's over. Spain has changed for good'], reimagines Jiménez's voice through a polyphony of women of different ages, ethnicities and professions (RTVE, 2023). The video begins with individual voices singing the refrain in isolation, their tones unaccompanied, almost tentative. Gradually, new timbres and faces join in – workers, students, older women and teenagers – until the fragmented voices merge into a chorus. The accumulation of sound mirrors the formation of collective identity, transforming solitude into solidarity and memory into action. At the visual level, the film reinforces this sonic crescendo. Each cut draws the viewer closer to the participants' faces, capturing breath and emotion rather than polished performance. The camera lingers on gestures – hands clasped, eyes closed and mouths opening in unison – while the original rumba rhythm fades beneath the layered voices. The absence of instrumental accompaniment foregrounds the corporeality of singing, as breath and timbre become instruments of presence. As the chorus builds, the images shift from domestic interiors to public spaces, evoking the passage from private endurance to public declaration that had already defined Jiménez's performance. The final scene shows a young girl wearing the Spanish women's football jersey. She stands silently, looking straight into the camera before the closing line appears on screen: 'Se acabó. Ahora ya España es otra'. This image encapsulates the campaign's message: the future belongs to a generation that has inherited the feminist struggles of the past but refuses to reproduce its silences. The girl's stillness echoes Jiménez's own composure in 1978, as both embody the same gesture of defiance, transformed by time.

The digital mobilisation of #SeAcabó can be understood as an extension of embodied feminist politics into virtual space. As Núñez Puente (2023) argues in her analysis of affect and feminist digital activism in Spain, online networks increasingly operate as arenas where collective emotions become catalysts for political mobilisation. The viral echo of #SeAcabó transforms affect into activism, translating the memory of resistance into digital resonance. What was once shouted in the streets is now amplified through networks and screens, where repetition, rhythm and shared indignation forge an immediate, participatory, and transnational feminist archive. In the Spanish context, this process acquires a distinctly sonic dimension as the feminist resonance of #SeAcabó bridges digital and musical spheres, transforming collective emotion into a shared affective politics of listening, visibility, and belonging.

7. CONCLUSION: GENDER JUSTICE THROUGH SOUND

Across the last five decades, Spain's confrontation with gender-based violence has unfolded through intersecting terrains – legal, political, cultural and affective. As shown throughout this chapter, feminist music cannot be separated from these broader struggles. From the juridical advances of the 2004 gender-based violence law and the 'Only Yes Means Yes' reform to the academic and activist efforts to name and analyse femicide, Spain has witnessed an expanding field of responses to machista violence. Scholars, artists and institutions have each contributed to making visible the structures that sustain gender inequality and to reimagining justice beyond the courtroom.

The study of music within this context – particularly feminist and memory-oriented approaches developed in recent decades – reveals how sound participates in this broader project of justice. Songs and performances act as archives of affect, allowing experiences of trauma, silencing and resistance to be collectively processed and transmitted. From early works that exposed the silencing of victims to contemporary analyses of popular music and reggaetón, these cultural practices evidence the essential role of listening, embodiment and voice in the feminist struggle against femicide. Music does not merely accompany these social and political transformations; it shapes them.

Drawing on the theoretical perspectives of Ahmed (2004, 2010), Butler (1990), Jelin (2002), Hirsch (2012) and Segato (2013), this chapter traced how memory, affect, embodiment and performativity intersect through musical practices. Each historical moment explored – from María Jiménez's 'Se acabó' and the punk defiance of Las Vulpes to Rozalén's 'La Puerta Violeta', the chants of 8M and the digital resonance of #SeAcabó – reveals how voice and rhythm function as carriers of feminist memory. Following Butler's (1990) theorisation of gender as performative, these sonic practices expose how repeated acts, gestures and vocal expressions materialise feminist resistance in public space. In turn, Ahmed's affective economies, Jelin's social memory work, Hirsch's postmemory and Segato's notion of justice from below converge to show how sound converts private injury into collective assertion. Within this constellation, feminist music also enacts what Rigney (2018) terms remembering hope, understood as a forward-looking form of memory work that sustains political imagination and future-oriented mobilisation. These sonic practices recall past violence and anticipate the world still to be built. Similarly, the circulation, reactivation and resignification of songs across generations exemplify Erll's notion of travelling memory (2011), a mobility that allows musical testimonies to move across time, bodies and political contexts, connecting the Spain of the late 1970s with the digital feminisms of the 21st century. The resurgence of 'Se acabó' during the #SeAcabó mobilisations is the clearest example of this transformation, whereby a personal rupture becomes, decades later, a collective outcry and a renewed demand for justice.

Meanwhile, feminist music from Latin America has profoundly influenced Spain. Vivir Quintana's 'Canción sin miedo' ['Song Without Fear'],

Ana Tijoux's 'Antipatriarca' ['Anti-Patriarch'] and Rebeca Lane's 'Nos Queremos Vivas' ['We Want Ourselves Alive'] address femicide, patriarchy and structural discrimination. These songs raise awareness in their countries of origin and have been incorporated into Spanish marches, cultural events and playlists, sensitising the public to gender-based violence. Performative phenomena such as 'Un violador en tu camino' ['A Rapist in Your Path'] by Las Tesis demonstrate how feminist art can go viral globally, including in Spain, fostering transnational dialogue on sexual violence, memory and collective resistance. Together, these artists and performances illustrate how music and performance can build cultural and political bridges between Latin America and Spain, reinforcing the struggle for women's rights and the visibility of gender-based violence on a global scale.

Yet, as the chapter has shown, music is also a terrain of dispute. The far right has attempted to harness musical performance to reinforce nationalist, misogynistic and racist narratives. Groups aligned with Vox, including Los Meconios and Infovlogger, have produced songs that reference the Francoist past and deploy discriminatory or demeaning language towards LGBTQ+ communities, feminist activists and racialised groups (González, 2022). Their material includes calls to return to the era of the 1936 military uprising, mockery of LGBTQ+ rights organisations framed through the idea of 'acceptable' versus 'unacceptable' homosexuality, and dismissive responses to cases of sexual violence when the victims or perpetrators are racialised. These examples show that music can serve both as a tool of resistance and as a vehicle for promoting sexist ideologies. The juxtaposition of feminist and ultra-right musical expressions highlights the contested cultural terrain over gender norms and social values in contemporary Spain.

Through the interweaving of memory, affect and performance, music creates spaces to confront violence, resist erasure and imagine repair. Even as new forms of backlash emerge, these sonic archives ensure that the cry of 'Not One More' continues to resound – an unfinished chorus of justice, remembrance and resilience, carrying the memory of past and present violence towards a horizon of collective hope.

REFERENCES

Ahmed, S. (2004). Affective economies. *Social Text*, *22*(2), 117–139. https://doi.org/10.1215/01642472-22-2_79-117

Ahmed, S. (2010). *The promise of happiness*. Duke University Press.

Álvarez-Benavides, R., & Jiménez-Aguilar, R. (2020). Estrategias de comunicación de la nueva extrema derecha española: De Hogar Social a Vox, del alter-activismo a la doctrina del shock. *Revista Latinoamericana de Estudios de la Paz y el Conflicto*, *1*(2), 55–78.

Amorós, C. (2006). *Conceptualizar es politizar. Conferencia inaugural en las Jornadas Sin equívocos: Violencia de género y otras formas de violencia en el seno de las familias, Madrid, 17–18 de noviembre de 2004* (pp. 19–30). UNAF en colaboración con el Ministerio de Asuntos Sociales.

Amorós, C. (1990). Violencia contra las mujeres y pactos patriarcales. In En V. Maquieira & C. Sánchez (Eds.), *Violencia y sociedad patriarcal* (pp. 39–53). Editorial Pablo Iglesias.

Araüna, N., Tortajada, I., & Figueras-Maz, M. (2020). Feminist reggaeton in Spain: Young women subverting machismo through 'Perreo'. *Young*, *28* (1), 32–49. https://doi.org/10.1177/1103308819831473

Arévalo, K., Chellew, E., & Figueroa-Cofré, I. (2018). Ni pobre diabla, ni candy: Violencia de género en el reggaetón. *Revista de sociología*, *33*(1), 7–23. https://doi.org/10.5354/0719-529X.2018.51797

Arias Salvado, M. (2021). Esto va a durar dos veranos: Pachangueo, inmigración latinoamericana y asimilación del reggaetón en la España de los 2000. En A. I. Queipo (Ed.), *El reguetón como movimiento cultural.* Dykinson.

Arroyo, J. (2022). La música de Rozalén recuerda a Ana Orantes 25 años después de su asesinato. *El País.* 17 de diciembre. https://elpais.com/sociedad/2022-12-17/la-musica-de-rozalen-recuerda-a-ana-orantes-25-anos-despues-de-su-asesinato.html

Bargueño, M. Á. (2019). *Las chicas son rockeras: El poder femenino en la música.* Ediciones Cátedra.

Bas-Peña, E., & Pastor-Bravo, C. (2024). Violencia de género y violencia sexual en las canciones de reggaetón: Estudio cualitativo. Pedagogía Social. *Revista Interuniversitaria*, *45*, 81–97. https://doi.org/10.7179/PSRI_2024.45.04

Bodelón, E. (2014). Violencia institucional y violencia de género. *Anales de la Cátedra Francisco Suárez*, *48*, 131–155. https://doi.org/10.30827/acfs.v48i0.2783

BOE. (2004). Ley Orgánica 1/2004, de 28 de diciembre, de Medidas de Protección Integral contra la Violencia de Género. *Boletín Oficial del Estado*, 21760.

BOE. (2010). Ley Orgánica 1/2010, de 2 de julio, de reforma del Código Penal. *Boletín Oficial del Estado, 152*, 53362–53431.

BOE. (2015a). Ley Orgánica 1/2015, de 30 de marzo, de modificación del Código Penal. *Boletín Oficial del Estado, 75*, 26523–26562.

BOE. (2015b). Ley Orgánica 8/2015, de 22 de julio, de modificación del Código Penal para la protección de menores y adolescentes frente a la violencia de género. *Boletín Oficial del Estado, 176*, 59347–59369.

BOE. (2015c). Ley 26/2015, de 28 de julio, de modificación de la Ley de Protección Jurídica del Menor y de medidas contra la violencia de género. *Boletín Oficial del Estado, 181*, 62478–62492.

BOE. (2017). Pacto de Estado contra la Violencia de Género. *Boletín Oficial del Estado, 301*, 121459–121480.

BOE. (2022). Ley Orgánica 10/2022, de 6 de septiembre, de garantía integral de la libertad sexual (Ley "Solo Sí es Sí"). *Boletín Oficial del Estado, 216*, 120554–120614.

Boneta, N., García, E., & Tomás, S. (2024). Culpables hasta que se demuestre lo contrario: Percepciones y discursos de adolescentes españoles sobre masculinidades y violencia de género. *Fundación Fad Juventud*. https://www.inmujeres.gob.es/publicacioneselectronicas/documentacion/Documentos/DE1962.pdf

Bosch, E., Ferrer, V. A., & Alzamora, A. (2006). *El laberinto patriarcal: Reflexiones teórico-prácticas sobre la violencia contra las mujeres*. Anthropos Editorial.

Bosch, E., Ferrer, V. A., & Gili, M. (1999). *Historia de la misoginia*. Anthropos.

Butler, J. (1990). *Gender trouble: Feminism and the subversion of identity*. Routledge.

Cabezas Fernández, A. (2023). *La reacción patriarcal: Saberes críticos y feministas ante el autoritarismo global*. Bellaterra.

Campillo, I. (2019). 'If we stop, the world stops': The 2018 feminist strike in Spain. *Social Movement Studies, 18*(2), 252–258. https://doi.org/10.1080/14742837.2018.1556092

Cappelle, A. (2023). *Collapse feminism: The online battle for feminism's future*. Repeater Books.

Carballo Villagra, P. (2006). Reggaeton e identidad masculina. *Cuadernos Inter.cambio sobre Centroamérica y El Caribe*, *3*(4), 83–94. https://www.redalyc.org/pdf/4769/476948766005.pdf

Casanovas-Buliart, L., Álvarez-Cueva, P., & Castillo, C. (2024). Evolution over 62 years: An analysis of sexism in the lyrics of the most-listened-to songs in Spain. *Cogent Arts & Humanities*, *11*(1). https://doi.org/10.1080/23311983.2024.2436723

De Miguel, M. (2004). *Ellas dan la nota: la aventura de la Plataforma de Mujeres Artistas contra la Violencia de Género*. Plaza & Janés.

Del Valle, C. (1999). *Amistades peligrosas*. https://www.amistadespeligrosas.miswebs.org/index.php/biografia/cristina-del-valle

Del Valle, C. (2025, 19 de agosto). Tenemos una sociedad machista y misógina donde las mujeres estamos en la periferia de los derechos. *Salud a Diario*. https://www.saludadiario.es/servicios-sociales/cristina-del-valle-tenemos-una-sociedad-machista-y-misogena-donde-las-mujeres-estamos-en-la-periferia-de-los-derechos/

Delegación del Gobierno contra la Violencia de Género. (2024, Noviembre). *Principales datos sobre violencia de género*. https://violenciagenero.igualdad.gob.es/wp-content/uploads/Principales_datos_noviembre_2024.pdf

El, Confidencial (2018, March 9). *'A la huelga', la canción que puso los pelos de punta en la manifestación feminista de Bilbao*. https://www.elconfidencial.com/espana/2018-03-09/huelga-cancion-letra-8marzo-paro-feminista-bilbao_1533125/

El País. (1983, Abril 28). *TVE considera 'hipócritas' las críticas a la canción de Las Vulpes*. https://elpais.com/diario/1983/04/28/radiotv/420328803_850215.html

El País. (1997, de diciembre 31). *Asuntos Sociales aboga por más protección para las mujeres maltratadas*. https://elpais.com/diario/1997/12/31/espana/883522819_850215.html

Erll, A. (2011). Travelling memory. *Parallax*, *17*(4), 4–18. https://doi.org/10.1080/13534645.2011.605570

Espinal Ramírez, L. F., Díaz-Fernández, S., & Orejuela, J. (2024). Tendencias investigativas sobre el reggaetón y horizontes de conocimiento futuro de un fenómeno sociocultural en expansión. *Cuadernos de música iberoamericana*, *37*, 415–444. https://doi.org/10.5209/cmib.99810

Europa Press. (2017). *Cristina Del Valle reconoce que es víctima de la violencia de género*. Recuperado de. https://www.europapress.tv/reportajes/342510/1/cristina-valle-reconoce-victima-violencia-genero

Fagoaga, C. (1994). Comunicando violencia contra las mujeres. *Estudios sobre el Mensaje Periodístico*, *1*, 67–82.

Fagoaga, C. (1999). La representación de la violencia: Maltrato en la pareja y agresión sexuada. *Hojas de Warmi*, *1*(1), 1–15. https://revistas.um.es/hojasdewarmi/article/view/166841/145051

Falcón, L. (1991). *Violencia contra la mujer*. Vindicación Feminista Publicaciones.

Faraldo-Cabana, P. (2021). The Wolf-Pack case and the reform of sex crimes in Spain. *German Law Journal*, *22*(4), 1–20. https://www.cambridge.org/core/journals/german-law-journal/article/wolfpack-case-and-the-reform-of-sex-crimes-in-spain/04D0A30DB36F9C1E3FE4C03DA246DF1E

Fenoy, B. (2018). *Ella [She]* [Song].

Forti, S. (2021). *Mitos y cuentos de la extrema derecha*. Catarata.

Gómez Escarda, M., Hormigos Ruiz, J., & Perelló Oliver, S. (2019). El ciclo de la violencia contra las mujeres en las canciones de música popular en España. *Andamios*, *16*(41), 331–353.

González, M. (2022, de octubre 9). *Un grupo musical invitado al festival de Vox canta "Vamos a volver al 36"*. El País. https://elpais.com/espana/2022-10-09/uno-de-los-grupos-musicales-invitados-al-festival-de-vox-en-madrid-canta-vamos-a-volver-al-36.html

González, D. (2023). *Reggaetón feminista: Perreo como herramienta de autoempoderamiento*. The Latinx Project. https://www.latinxproject.nyu.edu/intervenxions/reggaeton-feminista-perreo-as-a-tool-for-self-empowerment

Gordillo de Paz, M., & Manganas, N. (2025). "Telling the Truth to Stay Alive." stories of gendered violence and testimonial politics. In *The politics of gendered life stories in Spain: From private lives to public revolution* (pp. 25–56). Springer Nature Switzerland.

Hirsch, M. (2012). *The generation of postmemory: Writing and visual culture after the Holocaust*. Columbia University Press.

Hormigos-Ruiz, J., Gómez-Escarda, M., & Perelló-Oliver, S. (2018). Música y violencia de género en España. Estudio comparado por estilos musicales. *Convergencia*, *25*(76), 75–98.

Idoiaga Mondragón, N., Berasategi Sancho, N., Beloki Arizti, B., & Belasko Txertudi, A. (2020). Women's protests and the 8M movement in Spain: Mobilisation, identity, and collective action. *Social Movement Studies*, *19* (5–6), 633–650. https://doi.org/10.1080/09589236.2021.1881461

Informe España. (2023). *Feminicidios y otros asesinatos de mujeres*. https://feminicidio.net/wp-content/uploads/2023/11/INFORME-FEMINICIDIOS-2022-LR-1.pdf

Jelin, E. (2002). *Los trabajos de la memoria*. Siglo XXI Editores.

López Díez, P. (2003). La violencia contra las mujeres en los medios de comunicación. En *I Foro Nacional: Mujer, violencia y medios de comunicación* (pp. 91–100). Instituto Oficial de Radio y Televisión.

Laborde, A. (2019, julio 29). *Revolución en Puerto Rico a ritmo de reguetón*. El País. https://elpais.com/elpais/2019/07/29/gente/1564414757_656338.html

Lagarde y de los Ríos, M. (2005). *Los cautiverios de las mujeres: madresposas, monjas, putas, presas y locas* (2nd ed.). Universidad Nacional Autónoma de México.

Larumbe Gorraiz, M. Á. (2004). *Las que dijeron no: palabra y acción del feminismo en la Transición*. Universidad de Zaragoza.

Lorente Acosta, M., García, M., & Pérez, J. (2005). La violencia de género y sus consecuencias en la salud física y psicológica de las mujeres. *Revista Española de Salud Pública*, *79*(3), 345–357.

Maquieira, V., & Sánchez, C. (1990). *Violencia y sociedad patriarcal*. Editorial Pablo Iglesias.

Marcos, J. (2020, 6 de marzo). Las Vulpes, 37 años después: La autora de 'Me gusta ser una zorra' recuerda cómo una canción hizo temblar al país. *El País*. https://elpais.com/elpais/2020/03/06/icon/1583482433_220535.html

Menéndez Menéndez, M. I. (2016). Sin noticias de la LOPIVG: Los medios de comunicación y la publicidad una década después de la aprobación de la Ley Integral. En C. R. Orgaz & A. M. Romero Burillo (Eds.), *La protección de la víctima de violencia de género: un estudio multidisciplinar tras diez años de la aprobación de la ley orgánica 1/2004* (pp. 107–136). Editorial Tirant lo Blanch.

Menéndez Menéndez, M. I. (2010). *Representación mediática de la violencia de género: Análisis de la prensa balear (2004–2008)*. Edicions Universitat de les Illes Balears.

Ministerio de Igualdad. (2024). *Informes anuales del Observatorio Estatal de Violencia sobre la Mujer*. https://violenciagenero.igualdad.gob.es/violenciaencifras/observatorio/informesanuales/

Ms Nina. (2017). *Fresita* [Single]. La Vendición Records.

Muez, J. (1988, March 12). Denuncia por incitación a la violación a Los Ronaldos. *El País*. https://elpais.com/diario/1988/02/08/sociedad/571273204_850215.html#:~:text=incitaci%C3%B3n%20a%20la%20violaci%C3%B3n.La%20decisi%C3%B3n%20de%20interponer,se%20han%20celebrado%20el%20pasado%20fin%20de

Navarro, C., & Coromina, Ò. (2020). Discussion and mediation of social outrage on Twitter: The reaction to the judicial sentence of La Manada. *Revista Española de Sociología*, *29*(1), 45–66. https://doi.org/10.15581/003.33.37295

Núñez Puente, S. (2025). From #YoSíTeCreo to #SeAcabó: An exploration of the traces of the mobilization of rage in feminist digital activism in Spain. *Feminist Theory*, *0*(0). https://doi.org/10.1177/14647001251371967

Pastor-Gosálbez, I., Belzunegui-Eraso, Á., & Calvo Merino, M. (2021). La violencia de género en España: Un análisis quince años después de la Ley 1/2004. *Revista Espanola de Investigaciones Sociologicas*, *174*, 109–128. https://doi.org/10.5477/cis/reis.174.109

Pérez, J. (2014). Queer traces in the soundtrack of la Movida. In W. J. Nichols & R. Song (Eds.), *Back to the future: Towards a cultural archive of la Movida* (pp. 135–154). Fairleigh Dickinson University Press.

Pérez Villalba, E. (2007). *How political singers facilitated the Spanish transition to democracy, 1960–1982: The cultural construction of a new identity*. Edwin Mellen Press.

Ramírez, M. (2023, 28 Aug). *#MeToo exposed the abuse of women in Spain. It took football and #SeAcabó to spark a revolution*. https://www.

theguardian.com/commentisfree/2023/aug/28/me-too-women-spain-football-se-acabo-jenni-hermoso

Rigney, A. (2018).. *Remembering hope: Transnational activism beyond the traumatic. Memory Studies, 11*(3), 368–380. https://doi.org/10.1177/1750698018771869

Rivera, R. Z. (2009a). *Reggaeton.* Duke University Press.

Rivera, R. Z. (2009b). Policing morality, mano dura stylee: The case of underground rap and reggae in Puerto Rico in the mid-1990s. In En R. Z. Rivera, W. Marshall, & D. Pacini Hernández (Eds.), *Reggaetón* (pp. 99–120). Duke University Press.

Rodríguez, M. (2021). *Cómo ser Mala.* Planeta.

Ronaldos, L. (1987). *Sí, sí [Song].* EMI Music.

Rozalén. (2017). *La puerta violeta.* https://www.rozalen.org/2017/11/24/rozalen-estrena-el-video-de-la-puerta-violeta-un-himno-contra-la-violencia-de-genero/

RTVE Archivo. (1978, Octubre 3). *María Jiménez – Se acabó (Actuación en TVE 1978)* [Video]. YouTube. https://www.youtube.com/watch?v=av44ve-C2Ag

RTVE. (2023, 16 Nov). *Igualdad homenajea a María Jiménez en su campaña del 25 N: "Ahora ya España es otra".* https://www.rtve.es/noticias/20231116/campana-igualdad-25n-ahora-espana-ya-otra/2461070.shtml

Ruiz Castillo, A. (2006). *Las mujeres en la España contemporánea: educación sentimental y cultura patriarcal.* Cátedra.

Russell, D. E. H. (1976, March). The politics of femicide. *Paper presented at the International Tribunal on Crimes Against Women, Brussels, Belgium.*

Russell, D. E. H. & Radford, J. (Eds.) (1992), *Femicide: The politics of woman killing.* Twayne Publishers.

Segato, R. L. (2013). *La guerra contra las mujeres.* Traficantes de Sueños.

Snape, J., & Kassam, A. (2023, Agosto 21). Spanish football president's kiss sparks outrage after Women's World Cup final. *The Guardian.* https://www.theguardian.com/football/2023/aug/21/luis-rubiales-kiss-outrage-spanish-football-fa-president-womens-world-cup-final-spain-jenni-hermoso

Taylor, D. (2003). *The archive and the repertoire: Performing cultural memory in the Americas*. Duke University Press.

Uribe-Molina, J. (2022). Sin perreo no hay revolución? *Cambios Y Permanencias*, *13*(1), 327–343.

Usoz de la Fuente, M. (2015). *Urban space, identity and postmodernity in 1980s Spain: Rethinking the Movida*. Routledge.

Valiente Fernández, C. (2006). *El feminismo de Estado en España: El Instituto de la Mujer (1983–2003)*. Universitat de València.

Vanity Fair España. (2016, 24 de junio). *A quién le importa, 30 años después: así se gestó un clásico*. https://www.revistavanityfair.es/poder/articulos/historia-de-la-cancion-a-quien-le-importa-letra-nacho-canut/22532

Watkins, S. (2018). Which feminisms? *New Left Review*, *109*, 5–36. https://doi.org/10.64590/hli

Zavala, C. (2025, February 7). 'Ya no soy esa', la versión del clásico de Mari Trini con el que se ha atrevido Ona Mafalda. *Ya me siento esa mujer empoderada. Los 40*. https://los40.com/2025/02/07/ya-no-soy-esa-la-version-del-clasico-de-mari-trini-con-el-que-se-ha-atrevido-ona-mafalda-ya-me-siento-esa-mujer-empoderada/

3

SOUNDING THE ALARM: THE ROLE OF MUSIC IN SHAPING PUBLIC DISCOURSE ON FEMICIDES IN GREECE

ABSTRACT

This chapter examines the role of music in shaping public discourse on femicide in contemporary Greece. Centring on the murders of Eleni Topaloudi (2018) and Caroline Crouch (2021), it argues that, in the absence of robust legal recognition of femicide, popular music has become a vital medium through which grief, anger and solidarity are expressed and politicised. Drawing on case studies such as "Όλες απαντάμε αν αγγίξεις μία" ['We All Respond if You Touch One'] by Vivir Quitana and the Open Orchestra, Foivos Delivorias's 'Ελένη Τοπαλούδη' ['Eleni Topaloudi'], 'Καμία Μόνη' ['No One Alone'] by Spyros Grammenos and Nefeli Fasouli, 'Χιονάτη' ['Snow White'] by Thanos Papageorgiou and Kostis Amiridis and 'Τακούνια για Καρφιά' ['Heels for Nails'] by Orestis Dandtos, this chapter explores how artists transform mourning into mobilisation and the silence of subaltern voices *into sound. Using frameworks from feminist theory, affect studies and sound studies, including the work of Sara Ahmed, Judith Butler, Zizi Papacharissi and Brandon LaBelle, this chapter conceptualises music as a form of* acoustic citizenship, *that is, a practice through which citizens listen, grieve and act together. Ultimately, this chapter highlights how feminist music in Greece reclaims the cultural field as a site of resistance, rewriting silence into resonance and turning the demand for justice into a collective act of listening.*

Keywords: Femicide in Greece; feminist musical activism; affective publics; acoustic citizenship; grief and mobilisation; protest music; ethics of listening; feminist soundscapes

1. INTRODUCTION: FEMICIDES AND THE SOUND OF PROTEST

In recent years, Greece has witnessed an alarming rise in femicides: murders of women by men motivated by misogyny, control or possession. Though such crimes are neither new nor uniquely Greek, the scale, visibility and societal resonance of femicides in the last decade have triggered a reckoning that cuts across social, cultural and political domains. Two cases in particular have become emblematic of this national crisis. The 2021 murder of Caroline Crouch, a 20-year-old British woman killed by her husband, Babis Anagnostopoulos, in their Athens home, initially dominated headlines as a tragic home invasion. For more than a month, Anagnostopoulos played the role of bereaved husband, giving interviews and appealing for justice, until his eventual confession to the crime exposed a calculated deception. The revelation stunned the public and ignited a collective anger that extended beyond being directed at the perpetrator himself (Kogiou, 2025), towards the media, the justice system and the deeply entrenched patriarchal attitudes that sustain gender-based violence.

This case followed closely on the heels of the 2018 femicide of Eleni Topaloudi, a 21-year-old university student raped and murdered by two men on the island of Rhodes. The brutality of the attack and the subsequent media coverage, alternating between sensationalism and victim-blaming, shocked the nation and gave rise to widespread protests demanding justice. The trial, which concluded in 2020, was televised and discussed extensively across social media, turning Topaloudi into a symbol of both collective mourning and feminist mobilisation (Frantzi, 2024). The convergence of these two cases, each involving different perpetrators, contexts and media dynamics, revealed the structural continuity of gendered violence in Greece and its deep entanglement with cultural norms around masculinity, honour and control.

Despite public outrage and renewed calls from feminist organisations, Greece has yet to recognise femicide as a distinct legal category (Avramopoulou, 2025). Gender-based violence remains chronically underreported and insufficiently prosecuted (Karakasi et al., 2025). This gap between lived reality and institutional response has generated what might be termed a *cultural activism of grief and resistance*: a widespread turn to popular culture as a means of mourning victims, naming injustice and demanding change. In this climate, music has emerged as one of the most powerful platforms for social engagement.

Greek music has long been interwoven with the country's political and emotional life (Economou, 2018; Papadogiannis, 2014). From the rebetiko songs of the early 20th century, often described as the music of the dispossessed, to the protest songs of the dictatorship era and the socially conscious works of Mikis Theodorakis, music in Greece has historically acted as both chronicle and critique. It has voiced what institutions refused to articulate, offering solace, solidarity and dissent in times of silence or repression. In the 21st century, this legacy continues in the feminist outcry against femicide, where musicians have assumed the role of both mourners and agitators.

In the absence of comprehensive state or media frameworks for acknowledging the systemic nature of femicide, artists often turn their craft into acts of remembrance and protest (Asavei, 2019). Songs dedicated to women killed by men, whether explicitly named or symbolically invoked, have multiplied across genres, from contemporary *entechno* (a genre that blends elements of poetic lyrics, orchestral or even classical music influences and traditional Greek musical structures) and pop to rap, trap and folk hybrids. These compositions perform a dual function: they commemorate individual victims while simultaneously situating their deaths within a broader sociopolitical critique. For instance, lyrics and visual storytelling often juxtapose traditional gender imagery with scenes of violence, silence or revolt, foregrounding the cultural contradictions that enable femicide to persist.

Such songs have become more than aesthetic responses; they have evolved into cultural artefacts of collective mourning and resistance. They circulate widely through platforms such as YouTube, Spotify, Instagram and TikTok, transforming private grief into public discourse and amplifying feminist messages to audiences far beyond the reach of activist organisations (Proust, 2025). Listeners share, remix and comment on these works, forming what Zizi Papacharissi (2015) calls the bonds of *affective publics*: emotionally connected communities that mobilise around shared feelings of loss, anger and solidarity. In this way, music does not merely reflect public sentiment; it actively shapes it.

This chapter explores the intersection of music, gender-based violence and public discourse in contemporary Greece, focusing on how popular songs function as vehicles for awareness, critique and mobilisation around femicide. It argues that, in a sociopolitical context where legal recognition and media representation remain inadequate, music provides an alternative mode of feminist expression and civic engagement. Through rhythm, melody and lyrical narrative, artists reconstruct silenced stories, reclaim women's voices and invite listeners to bear witness.

The discussion unfolds in seven parts. Following this introduction, Section 2 contextualises the rise of femicide in Greece, examining the legal, cultural and media frameworks that have both obscured and enabled gender-based violence. It situates recent cases within broader debates about patriarchal norms, state response and the feminist movement's demand for legislative reform. Section 3 traces the historical lineage of Greek music as a form of social commentary, showing how the tradition of politically engaged songwriting provides the foundation for contemporary feminist musical activism.

Section 4 presents detailed case studies of musical responses to femicide, analysing how specific songs, ranging from *entechno* ballads to rap protest tracks, articulate grief, outrage and demands for justice. Through close readings of lyrics, musical composition and public reception, this section demonstrates how these works operate simultaneously as art, testimony and activism. Section 5 introduces the theoretical framework, drawing from feminist theory, affect studies and sound studies to conceptualise music as a site of emotional and political listening. Here, concepts such as Sara Ahmed's *feminist killjoy*, Judith Butler's *performativity* and Papacharissi's notion of *affective publics* are employed to examine how sound becomes a feminist act of resistance.

Section 6 synthesises the empirical and theoretical insights, arguing that the circulation of these songs transforms individual mourning into collective mobilisation. It considers how musical repetition, communal listening and participatory sharing foster a sense of belonging and political urgency among listeners. Finally, Section 7 concludes this chapter by reflecting on the implications of cultural activism in the struggle for gender justice, acknowledging both its transformative potential and its limitations in the face of systemic inertia.

By centring the role of music in the public conversation on femicide, this chapter highlights how cultural production can fill the void left by state inaction and institutional silence. Music, as a profoundly emotional and widely accessible medium, enables a form of civic participation grounded in empathy, remembrance and resistance. It turns listening into an ethical and political practice, one that insists on hearing the voices of those silenced by violence. In doing so, it reframes the act of mourning as a mode of protest and the act of singing as a declaration that *no woman's death will pass unheard.*

2. CONTEXT: FEMICIDES AND GENDER-BASED VIOLENCE IN GREECE

The visibility of femicide in Greece over the past decade has not emerged in a vacuum. It is the product of longstanding patterns of gender inequality, institutional neglect and a deeply entrenched patriarchal culture that shapes both social attitudes and legal responses to violence against women (Lomazzi, 2023). To understand how music has come to play a central role in articulating public outrage and mourning, it is necessary first to examine the broader context in which femicide occurs: the legal landscape, the media ecology that mediates public understanding of such crimes and the feminist movements that have challenged dominant narratives.

2.1 The Scope of the Problem

While accurate national data on femicide in Greece remain incomplete, available statistics paint a sobering picture. According to the European Institute for Gender Equality (EIGE), Greece has persistently scored below the EU average on gender-equality indicators, particularly in the domains of power and violence (Maricic & Jeremic, 2024). Data from the Hellenic Police and women's organisations such as Diotima Centre suggest that between 2019 and 2024, more than 50 women were murdered by current or former partners, family members or men motivated by sexual control or jealousy (Koureta et al., 2025). In 2021 alone, at least 17 femicides were reported (Papagiannopoulou, 2022), prompting Greek media to label it the year of femicides.

Despite this alarming trend, Greece has yet to introduce *femicide* as a distinct legal category (Avramopoulou, 2025). The criminal code continues to treat such murders as forms of homicide with intent, without recognising the gendered motivations that distinguish these crimes. Feminist organisations have repeatedly argued that this absence renders invisible the structural nature of gender-based violence, positioning each killing as an isolated act rather than as part of a continuum of coercion, abuse and misogyny. The debate intensified in 2022, when opposition parties proposed legislative amendments to include 'gender or gender identity' as aggravating factors in homicide cases. Yet, these were not adopted (EIGE, n.d.). The government's reluctance to define femicide legally reflects both political conservatism and a broader cultural discomfort with feminist language in public discourse.

2.2 Institutional and Legal Gaps

The Greek state has taken steps towards addressing domestic and gender-based violence, most notably through the ratification of the Istanbul Convention in 2018 (Niraki, 2023) and the introduction of Law 4531/2018 (Ranjan, 2020), which expanded the definition of domestic violence. However, implementation remains uneven. Police often fail to record domestic incidents properly, and survivors continue to encounter scepticism and secondary victimisation within the justice system. Shelters and support services, many of which depend on EU funding, are chronically under-resourced (Nikolaidou, 2025).

Legal scholars have pointed out that Greek criminal law's gender-neutral approach obscures the structural asymmetry between perpetrators and victims (Kyriakopoulou-Kollia, 2019). By refusing to name *femicide*, the system fails to acknowledge the social roots of these crimes in male entitlement and control. This linguistic and legal erasure mirrors the cultural silencing that feminist activism and cultural production seek to redress. The absence of gendered recognition within the law reinforces a *patriarchal realism* that treats violence against women as naturalised and private, rather than political and systemic (Ertürk, 2009).

2.3 Media Representations and Public Discourse

While the law has been slow to adapt, the media have played an ambivalent and often harmful role in shaping public perception (Kouroutsidou & Kakarouna, 2021). Greek television, newspapers and online platforms routinely sensationalise femicide cases, constructing narratives that oscillate between voyeurism and moral panic. Early coverage of Caroline Crouch's murder, for instance, focused on the supposed foreign intruders who had invaded the couple's home, reproducing xenophobic tropes until the husband's confession forced a narrative reversal. Even then, headlines framed the case through the psychology of the perpetrator, a man who lost control, rather than the systemic issue of male violence.

Similar patterns were evident in reporting on Eleni Topaloudi's case, where victim-blaming language and intrusive speculation about her personal life dominated the early coverage. Feminist media analysts have observed that such portrayals perpetuate a cultural script of the good versus bad victim: women who conform to moral expectations are mourned; those who deviate are implicitly blamed (Kourou & Athanasiades, 2022). This dichotomy not only distorts justice but also limits empathy, reinforcing the idea that some women are more deserving of protection than others.

The emergence of social media activism has partially disrupted this landscape. Hashtags such as #ΚαμίαΛιγότερη (Not One Less) and #γυναικοκτονία (femicide) became rallying points for digital mobilisation, particularly among younger generations. Feminist collectives, journalists and musicians began using Instagram, Twitter and YouTube to counter mainstream narratives, name victims and call for legal recognition. These online spaces laid the groundwork for what might be called an *alternative feminist public sphere* (McGuire, 2025), one that uses affect and solidarity to challenge institutional indifference. It is within this digital ecosystem that protest music has flourished.

2.4 Feminist Activism and Public Mobilisation

The years following the Topaloudi and Crouch murders saw an unprecedented wave of feminist organising in Greece. Demonstrations across Athens, Thessaloniki and Heraklion drew thousands of participants demanding justice and legislative change. Organisations such as Women's Rights Network and the Diotima Centre played key roles in documenting cases and providing legal aid to survivors.

Grassroots collectives, including To Μωβ (The Purple), adopted strategies that combined street protest with cultural production. Posters, murals, poetry and music were used to reclaim public space and visualise grief (Grammatikopoulou, 2025). The repetition of victims' names during marches became a ritual of remembrance, an embodied archive of absence and resistance. The slogan 'Δεν ήταν η ζήλια· ήταν η πατριαρχία' ('It wasn't jealousy; it was patriarchy') appeared across banners, graffiti and song lyrics, reframing intimate-partner violence as a societal structural issue rather than a private tragedy.

Importantly, feminist activism in Greece operates in tension with a wider social conservatism reinforced by the Orthodox Church and nationalist rhetoric. Public discussions of gender and sexuality often encounter moral panic and accusations of importing Western ideologies. This hostile environment heightens the importance of cultural interventions, especially music, that can reach audiences resistant to explicitly political discourse. Through melody and emotion, artists can communicate feminist messages in ways that transcend ideological boundaries.

2.5 The Cultural Turn: Music as Public Discourse

Against this backdrop of legal inertia and contested media narratives, music has emerged as a vital medium for articulating feminist anger and collective mourning. The transition from street protests to musical expression is not accidental but rooted in Greece's long history of using song as a vehicle for political consciousness (Papadogiannis, 2014). From the anti-dictatorship anthems of the 1970s to the socially critical lyrics of contemporary rap and *entechno* music, Greek audiences are accustomed to understanding music as a form of testimony and resistance.

In the wake of high-profile femicides, musicians have channelled public grief into art that speaks both to personal loss and systemic critique. Concerts and benefit performances dedicated to victims have become spaces of solidarity that merge the emotional and the political (Cayli, 2017). In many countries, songs explicitly referencing femicide circulate widely on digital platforms and are often accompanied by visual tributes that juxtapose the victims' faces with statistics on gender-based violence (Stetz, 2022). In doing so, they counter the fragmentary nature of news coverage, offering continuity and memory where institutional narratives have failed. In Greece, at the time of writing, such visual representation has not been observed. However, an increase in the circulation of songs referring to femicides or gender-based violence has been observed.

This cultural shift underscores a broader phenomenon: when political institutions and mainstream media fail to provide adequate frameworks for justice, popular culture becomes an arena for public reckoning. The feminist re-politicisation of Greek music can therefore be understood as part of a transnational movement, resonating with Latin American and Southern European contexts where art functions as both commemoration and resistance. Music's accessibility allows it to bypass linguistic, class and ideological barriers, engaging audiences who might otherwise remain detached from feminist discourse.

2.6 Towards a Sonic Understanding of Gender Justice

Understanding the significance of music in Greece's discourse on femicide requires a shift from viewing songs merely as artistic products to recognising them as *social acts of communication*. Through performance, musicians transform private pain into collective awareness, converting silence into resonance. This process echoes Judith Butler's (2009) notion of grievability, where public recognition of loss becomes a precondition for justice. In a society where many women's deaths are trivialised or depoliticised, musical memorialisation asserts that their lives, and deaths, matter.

The repetitive structure of song composition, with its choruses and refrains, invites participation and remembrance. Listeners become witnesses, joining a shared emotional community that transcends the boundaries of genre and geography. These dynamics prepare the ground for the next section, which explores how the historical tradition of politically engaged music in Greece has evolved into a distinctly feminist soundscape. By situating musical activism within this context of legal gaps, media distortion and grassroots mobilisation, we can better understand why the struggle against femicide in Greece is increasingly being fought not only in courts and parliaments but also in recording studios, concert halls and online playlists.

3. MUSIC AS SOCIAL COMMENTARY AND PROTEST IN MODERN GREECE

Music has long occupied a privileged place in the cultural and political life of Greece. From the subversive laments of *rebetiko* to the revolutionary songs of Mikis Theodorakis and the poetic compositions of Dionysis Savvopoulos, Greek music has repeatedly served as a channel through which society articulates dissent, solidarity and collective identity (Cowan, 1993). The enduring intimacy between music and politics, between sound and citizenship, provides the cultural foundation upon which today's feminist musical activism stands. Understanding this genealogy is essential to grasping how contemporary songs about femicide draw on, and transform, this tradition to confront gender-based violence.

3.1 Rebetiko and the Voices of the Margins

Often described as the 'Greek blues,' *rebetiko* emerged in the early 20th century from the urban underclass, refugees, workers and prisoners, who inhabited the fringes of Athenian society after the Asia Minor Catastrophe of 1922 (Tragaki, 2009). Sung in hash dens, taverns and dockside bars, *rebetiko* chronicled the challenging lives of the dispossessed: love, addiction, poverty, exile and incarceration. Because it gave voice to those excluded from official narratives, *rebetiko* was frequently censored by state authorities (Gerasopoulos, 2020), who regarded its lyrics and modes of expression as morally suspect.

Yet this very marginality endowed the genre with a profound political resonance. As Gail Holst-Warhaft (1998/2020) notes, *rebetiko* encoded a language of resistance, articulating the emotional life of communities living under constraint. The female figure in these songs, often portrayed as either the seductive betrayer or the tragic victim, reflected broader patriarchal attitudes but also hinted at the violence women endured within patriarchal structures (Holst-Warhaft, 2003). Modern feminist reinterpretations of *rebetiko* have sought to reclaim these voices, reimagining the *manges* (tough men) and *rebetisses* (female singers) as complex figures of gender negotiation.

In recent years, artists such as Giorgos Dalaras and the Ladies' Fingers Directing Duo have revived the rebetiko tradition to address contemporary issues, including domestic violence and femicide. Songs such as the 2025 song 'Ελενίτσα' ['Elenitsa'][1] (diminutive for Helen) and the 2021 reclaiming of the classic 'Τα Νέα της Αλεξάνδρας' ['Alexandras's News'][2] fuse the melancholic melodies of the old songs with feminist lyrics and contemporary instrumentation. They draw a historical continuum between past and present forms of suffering and resilience. The *rebetiko* lament, once a song of exile and poverty, becomes, in this new context, a lament for women silenced by patriarchal violence.

3.2 Theodorakis, the Dictatorship and the Politics of Song

The politicisation of Greek music reached its zenith during the period of military dictatorship (1967–1974). Mikis Theodorakis, already an established composer, transformed poetry into protest by setting the works of Yannis Ritsos, Odysseas Elytis and Giorgos Seferis to music. His songs, broadcast illegally and sung in secret gatherings, became emblems of resistance. The regime's attempt to suppress political expression only amplified the symbolic power of music as a space of free thought and emotional solidarity.

Theodorakis' use of melody and poetry as intertwined acts of resistance established a powerful precedent: that music could carry ideological weight equal to speech or print. The popularisation of political song during this era forged an enduring link between music and the moral conscience of the nation. As listeners sang along, they participated in an act of collective defiance.

For feminist artists working in today's Greece, this history provides both inspiration and contrast. Theodorakis' corpus largely framed resistance in national and class terms: women's experiences were marginal, their suffering often metaphoric rather than literal. Contemporary musicians expand the scope of protest to include gender-based injustice, thus reshaping the very definition of political song. The feminist turn does not reject the legacy of Theodorakis but rather radicalises it by applying its emancipatory ethos to the terrain of patriarchy and domestic violence.

3.3 From the Metapolitefsi to the Millennium: The Social Conscience of Entechno and Pop

The post-dictatorship period, known as the Metapolitefsi, witnessed an efflorescence of musical creativity (Papadogiannis, 2015). Artists such as Haris Alexiou, Eleftheria Arvanitaki, Alkistis Protopsalti and Nikos Xydakis infused *entechno* and popular music with reflective lyricism that addressed social change, migration and emotional endurance. Their songs combined the poetic tradition of earlier decades with a new intimacy, shifting from collective resistance to personal narrative.

Women performers, in particular, began to assert a distinct presence within the public sphere. Haris Alexiou's deep contralto and emotive delivery captured female experience in a male-dominated industry, while lyricists such as Lina Nikolakopoulou introduced a nuanced, feminist sensibility to Greek songwriting. Nikolakopoulou's collaborations with Alexiou, Arvanitaki and others produced some of the most introspective and socially conscious Greek songs of the 1980s and 1990s. Her lyrics often portrayed women as reflective, independent subjects negotiating love and social expectation, subtly challenging patriarchal norms.

This period also witnessed the emergence of music as commentary on rapid social transformations, economic liberalisation, urbanisation and European integration (Tsioulakis, 2020). The 1990s saw Greek pop artists, such as Anna Vissi, experimenting with global genres while maintaining a local social conscience. Music became a mirror of the contradictions of increasingly neoliberal times: prosperity and precarity, freedom and fatigue. Against this backdrop, feminist readings of popular songs began to gain traction, even if they were not always explicitly framed as such. By giving emotional voice to women's everyday struggles, these artists prepared the ground for a more overtly political feminist musical discourse in the 2000s and 2010s.

3.4 The New Millennium: Crisis, Identity and the Return of Protest

The financial crisis of 2008 and the subsequent decade of austerity re-politicised Greek culture. Songs once again became vehicles for protest, solidarity and identity formation. Emerging genres such as hip-hop, rap and trap, previously marginalised, gained mainstream visibility as youth turned to them for social commentary. Artists such as Στίχοιμα (Stihima), Social Waste and LEX used their platforms to denounce corruption, inequality and police violence. The language of protest shifted from poetic metaphor to raw realism, marking a generational change in the aesthetics of dissent.

This resurgence of political music coincided with the rise of digital platforms, which transformed how songs circulated and how audiences engaged. YouTube, SoundCloud and later TikTok enabled independent artists, especially women, to bypass traditional industry gatekeepers (Czaszewicz, 2024). Music videos, lyric videos and live sessions became accessible tools for social messaging. This technological democratisation fostered what might be termed a *participatory politics of sound*, where audiences no longer merely consumed protest music but actively shared, remixed and responded to it.

Feminist musicians seized this moment. Artists like Natassa Bofiliou, Mariza Rizou and Marina Satti began weaving gender critique into their work, using social media to articulate feminist positions on equality, consent and representation. Bofiliou's collaborations with lyricist Gerasimos Evangelatos, for instance, reimagined the *entechno* genre as a vehicle for progressive social commentary, while Rizou's playful performances often foreground women's agency and emotional autonomy.

Parallel to these mainstream artists, a younger generation of performers emerged within the rap and trap scenes, genres traditionally associated with hypermasculinity and misogyny, who began to challenge the sexism embedded within them. Female rappers such as Marseaux introduced lyrics that confronted harassment, victim-blaming and male entitlement. Their songs represent a crucial shift in a gendered musical hierarchy: they occupy spaces historically reserved for men and turn them into sites of feminist articulation.

3.5 Continuities and Ruptures: Feminist Reclaiming of the Political Song

The feminist engagement with music in contemporary Greece thus operates within a dialectic of continuity and rupture (Jameson, 2002). On the one hand, today's protest songs inherit the historical ethos of Greek musical resistance, the belief that melody and word can move the conscience of a nation. On the other hand, they mark a rupture by situating gender-based violence as a central political concern, rather than a private or secondary issue.

The continuity is evident in the persistence of collective motifs of contemporary songs: justice, dignity, memory and solidarity. Those addressing femicide echo the structural form of older political anthems: a slow build, a recurring refrain and an appeal to shared moral responsibility. Yet they rupture tradition by shifting the object of empathy: from the abstract 'people' or 'nation' to the individual woman whose life is threatened or actually was murdered. This reorientation personalises injustice, transforming national lament into feminist testimony.

In these feminist soundscapes, the private becomes public through the act of singing. As feminist musicologist Tia DeNora (2000) observes, music structures emotion and social action simultaneously; it shapes how individuals feel and how communities respond. In Greece, this has meant transforming domestic tragedy into civic urgency. Using victims' names in songs and performances functions as both memorial and indictment. It insists that the nation listen differently, that it hears the gendered dimensions of violence long naturalised or ignored.

3.6 Towards a Feminist Sonic Tradition

The evolution of Greek music from *rebetiko* subversion to feminist protest illustrates how cultural forms adapt to new struggles while retaining a recognisable political grammar. The *lament* (*mirologi*), a staple of Greek folk culture, resurfaces in songs about femicide as a vehicle for both grief and defiance. Where traditional laments were confined to the domestic sphere, sung by women to mourn the dead, contemporary feminist laments claim public space and political voice.

This recontextualisation marks the emergence of a *feminist sonic tradition*, one that fuses Greece's musical heritage of social commentary with a twenty-first-century urgency to name and resist gendered violence. It is a tradition that moves fluidly between genres and generations: from the smoky taverns of Piraeus to the digital stages of Instagram Live. In each instance, the act of singing carries ethical weight.

As such, music becomes not only a reflection of social change but also a participant in it. It mediates between the personal and the political, the past and the present, the silenced and the heard. In the context of femicide, these resonances acquire acute moral force: every verse, refrain and rhythm becomes a demand that women's lives be valued, remembered and protected.

4. CASE STUDIES: MUSICAL RESPONSES TO FEMICIDES IN GREECE

The past decade has witnessed an unprecedented intersection between feminist activism and musical production in Greece. While public debate about gender-based violence intensified following the murders of Eleni Topaloudi (2018) and Caroline Crouch (2021), artists across genres began using music to articulate collective grief, anger and defiance. These musical interventions not only commemorated the victims but also redefined the boundaries between art and activism, turning songs into public instruments of feminist consciousness-raising.

This section examines five distinct yet interconnected musical responses: 'Όλες απαντάμε αν αγγίξεις μία' ['We All Respond if You Touch One'], Foivos Delivorias's 'Ελένη Τοπαλούδη' ['Eleni Topaloudi'], 'Καμία Μόνη' ['No One Alone'] by Spyros Grammenos and Nefeli Fasouli, 'Χιονάτη' ['Snow White'] by Thanos Papageorgiou and Kostis Amiridis and 'Τακούνια για Καρφιά' ['Heels for Nails'] by Orestis Dandtos. Together, these works illuminate how Greek musicians, lyricists and listeners participate in an evolving movement that uses music to make femicide audible within public discourse.

4.1 'Όλες απαντάμε αν αγγίξεις μία' ['We All Respond if You Touch One']: Translating Resistance Across Borders

The Greek adaptation of the song *Canción sin Miedo*[3] was not a simple translation but a cultural re-composition. Its lyrics weave together the voices of Greek victims of femicide, naming them one by one.

Each name invokes a woman whose murder shocked Greek society: Eleni Topaloudi, Caroline Crouch, Tzebrie Hassan, Zak Kostopoulos (Zackie Oh), Maria, Anthi, Nektaria, among others. By interlacing these names with the refrain 'We all respond if you touch one,' the song constructs an explicitly political genealogy of violence and resistance. The cumulative naming turns grief into indictment, each verse a charge against 'system that washes them clean,' a phrase that condemns judicial leniency, media complicity and cultural normalisation of violence.

This *translingual act of protest* situates Greek feminism within a global continuum of resistance. While the Mexican and Greek versions share a structure of collective address and rhythmic urgency, the Greek rendition introduces a Mediterranean sensibility through melodic phrasing and choral texture. The performance by the *Ανοιχτή Ορχήστρα* is distinctly communal:

no single soloist dominates; instead, dozens of voices merge into a collective timbre that symbolises solidarity over individuality. The music video captures this ethos visually: faces of women singing in unison, intercut with images of protests, graffiti, and banners bearing victims' names.

Through this sonic and visual blending, 'Όλες απαντάμε αν αγγίξεις μία' embodies what cultural theorist Gayatri Spivak might call *translation as activism*, an act of carrying not just words but political affect across borders (Haroun, 2024). The adaptation does not mimic the Mexican original; it re-roots it in Greek soil, inflecting the global feminist anthem with local urgency.

The significance of this performance lies not merely in its lyrical content but in its collective enactment. The simultaneous singing by hundreds of participants across Greece transformed the event into a national soundscape of resistance (Mcteam, 2023). The performance video, released online the same day, rapidly went viral, shared by feminist organisations, media outlets and ordinary users. Each share amplified the same refrain, 'We all respond if you touch one,' until it became a declaration of collective identity and protection.

In feminist theory, collective singing operates as a form of embodied solidarity. As Judith Butler and Athena Athanasiou (2013) argue, the act of voicing together reclaims public space through vulnerability rather than force. In this case, the vulnerability of untrained voices singing outdoors, some trembling or breaking, underscores the authenticity of emotion. Their imperfect unison becomes a metaphor for feminist unity: diverse, polyphonic, yet coherent in purpose.

Moreover, the use of choral voice rather than solo performance in 'Όλες απαντάμε αν αγγίξεις μία' challenges patriarchal hierarchies of musical authority. The absence of a central star disrupts the traditional figure of the authoritative male singer who 'represents the people.' Instead, voice becomes plural and horizontal. The collective 'we' asserts that protection is reciprocal and networked, an ethic particularly resonant in Greece's small, interconnected feminist scene.

The performance also redefined the geography of protest in Greece. By dispersing performances across multiple cities, the organisers decentralised feminist activism, refusing the Athens-centric model of political action. In doing so, they transformed local squares, university courtyards and even village streets into *temporary feminist stages*. This spatial proliferation mirrored the song's message. Resistance is collective, ubiquitous and cannot be contained.

Sound studies scholars such as Brandon LaBelle (2018) emphasise that sound operates by occupying space differently than vision: it travels, overlaps and resonates. The 8 March 2022 performance exemplified this acoustic politics. Each local rendition became an echo of the others, creating a national resonance that no single performance could achieve. The result was not a unified concert but a dispersed chorus of belonging (Johnson, 2019), one that linked Greek listeners to the mothers of Oaxaca and to the broader global struggle against gendered violence.

Two years later, the video continues to circulate every International Women's Day, regaining momentum each time new cases of femicide are reported. Its endurance reflects both tragedy and necessity. Women continue to be murdered by partners, ex-partners or relatives, and Greece still lacks a legal category for femicide. In this context, 'Όλες απαντάμε αν αγγίξεις μία' remains not just a song but a living document of feminist persistence.

Its refrain, 'We all respond if you touch one,' has entered everyday speech, appearing on protest banners, social media captions and graffiti. Like the slogans of earlier movements ('Δεν ήταν η ζήλια, ήταν η πατριαρχία'), it condenses political analysis into visceral language. Each repetition renews a commitment: if patriarchy harms one woman, all are implicated in a movement of resistance.

The song's continuing relevance also attests to the power of transnational feminist exchange (Chakravarty, 2013). What began as a Mexican lament has become a Greek anthem, echoing in languages and contexts far removed from its origin yet united by shared structures of violence and solidarity. In this way, 'Όλες απαντάμε αν αγγίξεις μία' performs what scholar Chandra Talpade Mohanty (2003) calls *feminism without borders* – a politics that recognises difference but insists on interconnected struggle.

4.2 'Ελένη Τοπαλούδη': Naming a Life, Indicting a System

In 2021, acclaimed Greek songwriter Foivos Delivorias released a song that carries both the intimacy of a lament and the force of an indictment. Simply titled 'Ελένη Τοπαλούδη', it honours the 21-year-old university student raped and murdered on the island of Rhodes in 2018 by two men whose crime and trial became a national turning point in Greece's conversation about gender-based violence (Remoundou, 2022). The song, first performed live at the *Kyttaro Live Club* and later included in Delivorias's 2021 album *ANIME*, extends far beyond individual tribute. It stands as a meditation on justice, empathy and the social structures that enable femicide to persist.

In the four opening lines, Delivorias fuses image and indictment. The 'nets' evoke both the literal fishing nets used by her killers to conceal her body and the metaphorical nets of digital networks that first spread, and then sensationalised, her story. Thus, the song positions itself against the exploitative media spectacle surrounding the case, reclaiming narrative control from voyeuristic reporting.

By giving his song the victim's full name, Delivorias performs an act of re-individualisation (Flügel, 2018). In a media culture that tends to abstract victims into archetypes, the 'innocent student,' the 'jealous lover's victim', he insists on the specificity of a life lived and lost. The decision to title the piece *Eleni Topaloudi*, rather than using metaphor or anonymity, transforms the name into testimony.

Musically, *Eleni Topaloudi* follows Delivorias's signature *entechno* style: an elegant fusion of melodic lyricism and folk-inflected harmonic progressions. The instrumentation is sparse: guitar, piano and subdued percussion, allowing the voice to occupy intimate proximity to the listener. The tonal warmth of his delivery contrasts sharply with the brutality of the subject, treating beauty as a frame through which injustice becomes audible.

Delivorias's verses oscillate between mourning and critique. His lyrics evoke the impotence of language in the face of violence, while the imagery of flowers that 'see the sun and die' allegorises young women's thwarted potential. The poetic economy here intensifies emotional resonance.

Later verses turn outward, addressing institutional failure where irony replaces lament. The reference to the *Penal Code* indicts a justice system that, in many femicide cases, has been slow or reluctant to name gender as motive. By anticipating the institutional impulse to 'cancel' his words, Delivorias acknowledges his own position as a male artist entering a discourse dominated by women's voices. Rather than claiming authority, he uses irony to expose the distance between law and lived experience.

Unlike the choral activism of 'Όλες απαντάμε αν αγγίξεις μία', Delivorias's composition is deliberately solitary. There is no chorus of women's voices, no collective march. The setting is the intimate space of the singer-songwriter, a single male voice confronting complicity. This intimacy is strategic. It places responsibility squarely on the listener, particularly the male listener, inviting reflection rather than comfort.

The fact that 'Eleni Topaloudi' was written and performed by a male artist is significant. Delivorias participates in what Miriam Abelson (2014) terms *transformative masculinity*, a redefinition of manhood through accountability and care. His song thereby broadens the spectrum of feminist musical activism, demonstrating that solidarity need not erase difference.

In this regard, 'Eleni Topaloudi' complements rather than mirrors 'Όλες απαντάμε αν αγγίξεις μία.' Where the latter unites women's voices into a collective roar, Delivorias's track stages the silence of men who must learn to listen. The two together form a dialogue across gender: sound and echo, call and response.

Delivorias's 'Eleni Topaloudi' exemplifies how music can bear witness where institutions falter. It demonstrates the ethical potential of song to articulate grief in ways that neither journalism nor jurisprudence can. The track's quiet tone refuses the sensationalism that characterised media coverage of the case. Instead, it insists on dignity, attention and sustained empathy.

Through its minimalism, the song enacts an opening towards the other, transforming hearing into an ethical relation. In listening to 'Eleni Topaloudi,' the audience participates in an act of remembrance that transcends spectacle and enters the collective conscience.

4.3 'Καμία Μόνη' and 'Χιονάτη': Poetic Rage and Modern Laments

While songs such as 'Όλες απαντάμε αν αγγίξεις μία' and 'Ελένη Τοπαλούδη' channel collective mourning and ethical witness, other contemporary Greek compositions approach femicide through metaphor, allegory and tonal contrast. Two striking examples reveal how artists weave the aesthetics of Greek songwriting with the language of resistance: 'Καμία Μόνη' ['No One Alone'] by Spyros Grammenos and Nefeli Fasouli and 'Χιονάτη' ['Snow White'] by Thanos Papageorgiou and Kostis Amiridis. Both articulate outrage through poetic form, yet they differ sharply in effect: 'Καμία Μόνη' explodes in collective fury, while 'Χιονάτη' retreats into elegiac tenderness. Together they illustrate the expanding emotional spectrum of feminist musical response in Greece.

When 'Καμία Μόνη' appeared in 2022, it struck listeners as an anthem born of exhaustion and rage. Written by singer-songwriter Spyros Grammenos with music co-composed by Vasilis Dokakis, the song gives voice to a society reeling from successive femicides. The lyrics open in the tone of a love ballad, quickly twisting into rebellion:

The gentle imagery of scent and colour collapses as the song shifts key and rhythm, breaking into its refrain. The sudden escalation from mourning to militancy encapsulates what cultural theorist Raymond Williams called a *structure of feeling* (Matthews, 2001). That is, the shared pulse of an era where sorrow mutates into revolt. The refrain's final line, '*If I don't come back, burn the city*', is not hyperbole but quotation. It references slogans spray-painted by Greek feminists after several murders in 2021, echoing Latin American protest chants that threaten symbolic destruction as moral reckoning. By embedding this phrase within popular song, 'Καμία Μόνη' translates street protest into a sonic event accessible to wider audiences.

What distinguishes the piece is its fusion of intimacy and militancy. The first verses are personal, even romantic; the later ones are public and explosive. This shifting register mirrors the political argument that femicide is not an individual tragedy but the violent endpoint of everyday sexism. The song's energy rises until its end, where voices dissolve into feedback, a literal refusal of resolution. The absence of a final cadence leaves listeners suspended, an aural performativity of unfinished justice.

Where 'Καμία Μόνη' erupts in fury, 'Χιονάτη' ['Snow White'] whispers its critique through allegory. Written and composed by Kostis Amiridis and performed by Thanos Papageorgiou, the song borrows the imagery of a children's tale only to dismantle its illusions. Its opening verse evokes a dark nursery rhyme.

From the first lines, the romantic myths that once promised salvation – the kiss, the slipper, the prince – are inverted into instruments of harm. The fairy tale becomes a vehicle for social commentary. The danger comes not from witches or wolves but from 'men who look like angels and drip poison on the earth.' Amiridis's lyrics reveal how patriarchal ideals of romance mask the potential for violence, while the soft waltz rhythm and minor-key melody cloak the critique in melancholy beauty.

Midway through, the song enumerates names. Each name evokes another absent woman, echoing the naming strategies used in other feminist songs yet filtered through gentleness rather than protest. The repetition functions as a litany, aligning 'Χιονάτη' with Greece's long tradition of *μοιρολόι* (lament).

The choice of title deepens the irony. Snow White, the archetypal passive heroine who must be awakened by male desire, becomes here a figure of resistance through absence. She 'returns marked among the clouds,' her purity stained by the violence she has suffered. The subversion is subtle but pointed: the fantasy of rescue is revealed as lethal.

Papageorgiou's understated delivery enhances this quiet devastation. His voice, close-miked and tremulous, invites the listener into intimacy; there is no distance between singer and story. The arrangement – acoustic guitar, faint cello, minimal percussion – creates an atmosphere of domestic space, as though the song were being sung in a bedroom rather than a studio. The effect is chilling: violence has entered the most private realms of life and art alike.

Together, 'Καμία Μόνη' and 'Χιονάτη' demonstrate the plurality of feminist musical expression in Greece. Both respond to the same epidemic of femicide, yet they articulate different emotional and aesthetic strategies. 'Καμία Μόνη' externalises anger, transforming grief into collective energy. Its sonic vocabulary belongs to the tradition of protest song. 'Χιονάτη', by contrast, internalises sorrow, addressing listeners through the quiet intimacy of allegory. Its critique emerges not from volume but from inversion: the fairy-tale melody that turns sinister as the lyrics unfold. Where 'Καμία Μόνη' disrupts silence through noise, 'Χιονάτη' disturbs comfort through beauty. Both force listeners to confront violence in spaces where they expect harmony.

4.4 'Τακούνια για Καρφιά': From Stage Song to Social Ritual

Among the many songs that have entered Greece's growing archive of feminist sound, few have achieved the symbolic resonance of 'Τακούνια για Καρφιά' ['Heels for Nails']. Written by Orestis Dandtos and performed by Ioulia Karapataki, the song intertwines delicate melody with unflinching critique, transforming the image of the high heel, a traditional emblem of femininity, into a weapon of poetic justice. Its lyrics oscillate between tenderness and defiance, depicting women reclaiming public space, shedding fear and confronting 'the monster' that stalks them.

This imagery, simultaneously violent and liberatory, captures the song's dual function as lament and resistance. Yet what gives 'Τακούνια για Καρφιά' an enduring political life is not only its artistry but its afterlives in performance, particularly two moments when it was reinterpreted by communities outside the music industry: the 2024 memorial for Kyriaki Griva in Athens and the flash mob video by students at the Music School of Lamia. Each instance reveals how feminist music in Greece transcends entertainment to become civic ritual, education and collective therapy.

On 1 April 2024, outside the police station of Agioi Anargyroi, a small crowd gathered in grief and protest. It was the site where 28-year-old Kyriaki Griva was murdered by her former partner, a crime that, like so many others, had been preceded by reports of harassment and ignored warnings (Efthymiadou, 2025). During the unveiling of a memorial plaque, Kyriaki's mother stood before journalists, activists and neighbours and began to sing 'Τακούνια για Καρφιά' (The TOC Team, 2025).

The moment, captured in televised footage and widely shared on social media, stunned the nation. Her voice transformed the song into something profoundly different from its original recording. No longer a professional performance, it was a mother's invocation, an act of mourning that reclaimed both sound and space. The lyrics' prophetic lines, 'Soon she will go out into the city/without fear, without a hidden gun', echoed with unbearable irony, yet also with defiance.

In that performance, 'Τακούνια για Καρφιά' became a *sonic memorial*, linking the personal loss of one woman to the collective grief of a country. The scene outside the police station carried heavy symbolism. A site associated with protection and authority became, through music, a site of accusation. The mother's voice functioned as counter-testimony, an embodied protest against the failures of state institutions to safeguard women's lives.

The moment becomes an *acoustic counterpublic*: a space where those silenced by violence or bureaucracy reclaim audibility. Here, grief became political through the act of singing. The performance drew attention to how women's voices, often marginalised or dismissed as emotional, can carry the moral weight of truth.

Equally poignant was the choice of song. Though written by a male lyricist, 'Τακούνια για Καρφιά' had already been adopted by women's groups as an anthem of survival. By singing it, Kyriaki's mother not only honoured her daughter but also affirmed solidarity with all victims' families. The refrain '*να εκδικηθεί η ομορφιά*' ('for beauty to take revenge') resonated as both lament and threat, beauty here symbolising the dignity of women who refuse to vanish into silence. The moment encapsulated the transformation of song into civic ritual (Chaney, 1983), a theme increasingly central to Greece's feminist musical culture.

If the Agioi Anargyroi memorial expressed grief transfigured into protest, the Lamia flash mob of November 2023 exemplified music's pedagogical and mobilising potential. On 7 November, the AlBaTroS Choir and the rock ensemble of the Music School of Lamia gathered unexpectedly in Eleftheria Square to perform 'Τακούνια για Καρφιά'. It was part of a student-led awareness campaign against gender-based violence, filmed as a one-take video and shared widely online.

In this version, teenage voices and electric guitars replaced Karapataki's refined *entechno* aesthetic with youthful urgency. The performance opened quietly. One voice began the first verse a cappella as passersby paused. Then, as the drums entered, dozens of students joined in, forming a spontaneous chorus. The effect was both haunting and hopeful. The young performers' sincerity lent the song a new dimension of authenticity.

The symbolism of the flash mob was powerful. It occurred on 17 November, the anniversary of the 1973 Polytechnic Uprising, Greece's national day of student resistance. By choosing that date, the organisers implicitly linked the struggle against gendered violence to the country's historical memory of democracy and rebellion. In doing so, they reframed feminism not as a niche social issue but as part of the broader continuum of civic rights and human dignity.

Crucially, *Τακούνια για Καρφιά* served here as an educational tool. The teachers who supervised the event emphasised that music education must address social realities, not just artistic technique. Through this performance, students learnt not only harmony and rhythm but also empathy and social responsibility. The inclusion of both boys and girls in the ensemble symbolised collective accountability, a pedagogical enactment of the song's core message that violence against women concerns everyone.

The parallel between these two performances demonstrates how 'Τακούνια για Καρφιά' functions as more than a cultural text. It is a vessel for collective articulation (Agarwal, 2015). In both cases, music traverses boundaries between art and activism, private emotion and public space and grief and hope.

The mother's voice represents continuity with Greece's oral traditions of lament, where women sing the dead into memory; the students' chorus represents innovation, projecting that memory forward through digital media. Together, they embody a cycle of feminist transmission (Lamas, 2011), from one generation mourning to another learning, from silence to speech to song. In this sense, the song exemplifies the dual trajectory of Greek feminist music: it travels inward into personal experience and externally into collective action. Each time it is sung, it reconfigures the national soundscape of mourning and justice.

4.5 The Ethics of Listening

Across these examples, one theme recurs: the transformation of listening into an ethical and political practice. Listening becomes, in this sense, a form of civic responsibility. It entails acknowledging the humanity of victims, confronting one's complicity in systems of silence and sustaining attention when media cycles move on. The repetition of melodies and names highlights that political violence becomes part of everyday consciousness rather than an exceptional event. In the Greek context, where institutional silence persists, this recognition is both painful and necessary.

5. THEORETICAL FRAMEWORK: THE POLITICS OF LISTENING

The musical interventions examined in the previous section do more than express emotion or memorialise victims. They constitute political acts that reshape how violence, mourning and justice are collectively understood. To grasp the depth of their social significance, it is necessary to situate them within a broader theoretical framework that considers sound not simply as art but as a mode of feminist praxis (Ingleton, 2017). The intersection of feminist theory, affect studies and sound studies offers a rich conceptual vocabulary for interpreting these songs as forms of embodied resistance and as catalysts for what Sonevytsky (2016) called *acoustic citizenship*.

This section elaborates four interrelated concepts that illuminate how music operates as public discourse on femicide in Greece: (1) feminist affect and the ethics of emotion, (2) performativity and the politics of voice, (3) affective publics and networked solidarity and (4) acoustic citizenship and the ethics of listening. Together, they demonstrate how acts of singing, mourning and listening function as sites of political participation, transforming the aural into the ethical.

5.1 Feminist Affect and the Ethics of Emotion

Feminist theorists have long argued that emotion is not a private, apolitical phenomenon but a social force that structures relations of power and belonging. Sara Ahmed's *The Cultural Politics of Emotion* (2004) and *Living a Feminist Life* (2017) are foundational in this respect. Ahmed posits that emotions *stick* to bodies and objects, shaping how certain subjects become recognisable while others remain invisible. Anger, pain and sorrow, often dismissed as feminine or irrational, are thus forms of political knowledge that expose injustice.

Within the Greek context, songs such as 'Με Ποιο Δικαίωμα/Me Pio Dikeoma' ['By What Right'] with music composition and lyrics by Angeliki Vlachaki and Pelagia Kelidou transform these *sticky* emotions into collective energy. They mobilise *affective economies of grief and rage* to confront institutional apathy. When listeners weep, sing along or share these songs online, they participate in what Ahmed (2017, p. 198) calls *feminist snap*: a moment when affect breaks the social expectation of silence and compliance.

The emotional intensity of these songs is therefore not incidental but constitutive of their political power. Grief becomes a language of solidarity; anger becomes evidence of care. As feminist scholar Audre Lorde (1997, p. 280) famously declared, anger is 'loaded with information and energy.' Greek musical activism draws on precisely this energy, transforming the despair surrounding femicide into a collective insistence on visibility and justice.

At the same time, these emotional registers challenge dominant media portrayals that aestheticise women's suffering. Whereas mainstream news often sensationalises femicide through melodrama or voyeurism, feminist music reclaims emotion as ethical expression rather than spectacle. It invites *empathic recognition* (Schwaber, 1981); that is, a listening that feels with, rather than one that looks at. This shift from vision to audition, from gaze to listening, reorients the politics of witnessing towards the relational and the embodied.

5.2 Performativity and the Politics of Voice

If affect theory foregrounds the emotional dimension of feminist song, Judith Butler's theory of performativity provides insight into how these musical practices enact social transformation through repetition and embodiment. Butler (1999) argues that gender is not a stable identity but a performative effect produced through repeated acts, gestures and discourses. Likewise, resistance can be performed through the rearticulation of those acts: through speaking, singing or moving differently.

In *Notes Toward a Performative Theory of Assembly*, Butler (2015) extends this logic to collective action, proposing that public assembly itself is a performative claim to the right to appear. When bodies gather, whether in streets or online spaces, they assert their existence and interdependence. In the musical protests surrounding femicide in Greece, this performative claim is realised through sound. Singing or listening collectively becomes a way of making bodies audible when they are otherwise invisible within patriarchal institutions.

The performativity of music lies in its repetition and resonance. Each time the refrain 'Το Τραγούδι των Χαμένων Γυναικών'/'To Tragoudi Ton Hamenon Gynaikon' ['Song of the Lost Women'], music composition by Kallias Konstantinos and lyrics by Panagiotis Kevopoulos, is sung, it reiterates a feminist claim to presence. The voice operates here as both individual expression and communal signifier, a fusion of the singular and the plural. This duality destabilises the patriarchal separation of public and private spheres. What might once have been confined to the domestic lament (*mirologi*) now resounds in public squares and digital networks.

Butler's notion of *grievability* is also crucial. In *Frames of War* (2009), she argues that political hierarchies determine whose lives are deemed worthy of mourning. The recurring naming of victims in Greek protest songs directly confronts this hierarchy. Each name sung restores grievability, transforming the memory of women who might otherwise be reduced to news statistics into subjects of public mourning and remembrance. Through these performative acts, music creates an alternative *frame of recognition* (Steiner, 1982), one that insists on women's full humanity and social worth.

5.3 Affective Publics and Networked Solidarity

The rise of feminist musical activism in Greece cannot be separated from the digital infrastructures through which it circulates. Social media platforms, particularly YouTube, Instagram and TikTok, function as arenas of what Zizi Papacharissi (2015) terms *affective publics*: networked collectives mobilised by shared emotional intensities rather than formal organisation.

Unlike traditional social movements grounded in manifestos or institutions, affective publics operate through circulation, repetition and affective resonance. The hashtags #ΚαμίαΛιγότερη (Not One Less) and #γυναικοκτονία (femicide) exemplify this phenomenon in the Greek context. Each shared song, video or lyric becomes a node in an expanding web of emotional connection.

The significance of these affective publics lies not in their permanence but in their *embodied immediacy*. They enable rapid emotional alignment around events, such as a new femicide case, allowing outrage, sorrow and solidarity to coalesce almost instantly. In this way, the sharing of digital music functions as both expression and mobilisation. When users post clips of 'Τραγουδάμε Δίχως Φόβο' ['We Sing Without Fear'], a Greek version of 'Canción sin Miedo' with captions like 'for Eleni,' 'for Caroline' or simply 'for all of us,' they transform the act of listening into a micro-political gesture of remembrance.

Affective publics also democratise the production of meaning. Listeners remix songs, create subtitled videos or record their own covers, thereby expanding the interpretive field. This participatory dynamic aligns with Nancy Fraser's (1990) concept of *subaltern counterpublics*: parallel discursive arenas where marginalised groups generate and circulate counter-hegemonic narratives. Greek feminist musical activism exemplifies such a counterpublic, one sustained not by formal leadership but by affective exchange.

Yet affective publics are not without ambivalence. As Papacharissi (2015) cautions, they risk dissipating as quickly as they form, their emotional energy absorbed by algorithmic logics of attention. The challenge for feminist musical activism, therefore, is to convert fleeting virality into enduring cultural memory. This is where the materiality of music – the record, the live performance and the concerted chorus – anchors affect in shared experience, giving it longevity beyond the scroll of the feed.

5.4 Acoustic Citizenship and the Ethics of Listening

The final theoretical strand derives from sound studies, a discipline which examines, among other topics of meaning and media of circulation, how listening structures social relations. Scholars such as Brandon LaBelle (2018), Veit Erlmann (2020) and Jennifer Stoever (2016) have argued that sound operates as a medium of power: who is heard, who listens and under what conditions reveal the hierarchies of the public sphere. In patriarchal cultures, women's voices have historically been confined, policed or dismissed as noise. To sing about femicide, therefore, is not merely to make sound but to contest the very politics of audibility.

Maria Sonevytsky's (2019, p. 174) concept of *acoustic citizenship* is particularly illuminating. Sonevytsky proposes that individuals enact citizenship through acts of listening, voicing and sounding that claim participation in public space. Acoustic citizenship does not depend on legal recognition but on the sensory occupation of space through sound. In Greece, where official discourse has often muted feminist perspectives, music becomes a means of asserting presence: to sound is to belong.

This framework redefines activism itself. Whereas traditional political participation emphasises speech, sound studies remind us that listening is equally political. The feminist songs discussed earlier demand attentive listening – not the passive consumption of music but an ethical engagement that acknowledges pain and responsibility. Listening, in this sense, is a form of solidarity. It recognises the *relational vulnerability* (Bridgeman, 2013) that underpins feminist ethics, the awareness that one's own security is entangled with the safety of others.

Moreover, the sonic qualities of these songs – repetition, echo and resonance – enact this relationality. Sound, unlike sight, cannot be contained; it travels, surrounds and implicates the listener. When a crowd sings 'Τραγουδάμε Δίχως Φόβο'/'Tragoudame Dihos Fovo' ['We Sing Without Fear'] in Syntagma Square, the vibrations bind strangers into a temporary community. This acoustic collectivity mirrors what Jacques Rancière calls the *redistribution of the sensible* (Highmore, 2011) that is, the reconfiguration of what can be seen, said and heard within a given social order. By amplifying women's voices, these songs expand the auditory field of the political, making femicide audible where it was previously unspeakable.

Listening as an ethical practice also challenges the spectacularisation of violence (Lopez, 2018). In contrast to visual media's fixation on images of victims, sound invites proximity without voyeurism. It engages the listener's body: the heartbeat synchronises with the rhythm, the breath aligns with the melody, thus producing empathy through resonance rather than spectacle. This shift from seeing to hearing transforms the politics of witness from distant observation to embodied participation.

5.5 Intersections: From Emotion to Resonance

Taken together, these theoretical perspectives reveal the multilayered politics at work in Greek feminist music. Emotion, performance, network and sound converge to create a sonic public sphere (Michael, 2018) grounded in relational ethics rather than institutional authority. Emotion transforms silence into shared feeling, performance converts vulnerability into visibility, networked affect extends solidarity across digital space and acoustic citizenship situates listening as the foundation of belonging.

Within this constellation, music becomes a form of *feminist pedagogy* (Webb et al., 2002), teaching listeners how to feel, how to listen and how to act. Each repetition of a melody or lyric reinforces an ethical orientation towards the other, cultivating *engaged listening*, the capacity to remain open to discomfort, to be changed by hearing (Parks, 2018).

In the Greek struggle against femicide, this pedagogy operates both consciously and intuitively. A listener may not articulate Ahmed's or Butler's theories, but by singing along to Gerasimos Evangelatos's lyrics 'Δεν έχω μάθει δυστυχώς να μην ανήκω/Μια στο βοσκό, μια στο μαντρί και μια στο λύκο' ('I've never learned, alas, how not to belong/To the shepherd, to the flock, to the wolf)', they have the potential to perform the very ethics those theories describe. In this instance, the political emerges not from academic discourse but from the embodied practice of listening together.

5.6 Towards a Feminist Politics of Resonance

The politics of listening outlined here invites a reconceptualisation of how we understand activism in the age of digital culture. Traditional models emphasise speech, visibility and protest; the feminist sonic turn in Greece foregrounds resonance, audibility and listening as equally vital forms of participation.

Resonance operates both literally and metaphorically. Literally, it refers to the vibration of sound waves that connect bodies in shared space. Metaphorically, it signifies the echo of one life within another. In songs about femicide, resonance transforms personal tragedy into collective consciousness. The refrain, repeated across voices, performs solidarity through sound.

In this sense, music is not simply a mirror of social reality but an instrument of its reconfiguration (DeNora, 1995). By inviting listeners to feel, sing and listen differently, feminist musicians in Greece enact a reordering of the social sensorium.

The theoretical frameworks of affect, performativity and acoustic citizenship thus converge in a simple yet profound proposition. To listen is to care, and to care is to act. In a society where women's suffering has too often been met with silence, this ethics of resonance transforms the act of listening into an act of justice.

6. FROM MOURNING TO MOBILISATION

Music's capacity to bridge emotion and action, grief and protest, lies at the heart of its political power. In the Greek struggle against femicide, this bridging function has transformed what might otherwise have remained moments of private mourning into acts of collective mobilisation. Songs written for or inspired by murdered women, shared across public squares and digital networks, create spaces where sorrow becomes solidarity and sound becomes strategy. The transition from mourning to mobilisation is neither spontaneous nor inevitable. It is the result of a deeply cultural process in which affect is organised, amplified and sustained through music.

6.1 The Emotional Architecture of Mobilisation

As discussed in the preceding section, feminist music operates within an *affective economy* (Lehmann et al., 2019), in which emotions circulate between bodies, attaching listeners to political causes. This circulation is palpable in the wake of each femicide in Greece. Grief first manifests as shock and despair, then coalesces into anger and demand for political action. Music gives this movement both form and tempo. Through melody and rhythm, it offers emotional continuity across disparate experiences of loss.

Songs, such as those discussed in Section 4 of this chapter, provide listeners with a structure for feeling, an emotional script that validates pain while directing it outward. The repetition of choruses and refrains allows grief to be rehearsed and rearticulated until it becomes an organising principle rather than a paralysing one. The beat of the song synchronises the heartbeat of the collective. The voice of the singer becomes a proxy for the voices that cannot speak.

In feminist marches and vigils, this emotional architecture becomes palpable. As already discussed in Section 4.1, crowds singing together enact *performative assembly* (Butler, 2015), a gathering that asserts existence through shared vulnerability. The transition from listening privately to singing publicly marks the crossing point from empathy to activism. In that moment, music ceases to be an accompaniment to protest and becomes its medium.

6.2 Sonic Rituals of Resistance

Mobilisation around femicide in Greece often takes the form of *ritualised sonic acts*: vigils with candles and songs, performances where victims' names are read aloud or collective chants that transform the streets into acoustic corridors of grief. These rituals draw from both folk and religious traditions, the *mirologi*, the Orthodox requiem and even the secular protest song, reconfiguring them for feminist ends.

These musical rituals also challenge the temporality of grief. Whereas official memorials tend to close the narrative, marking death, then moving on, feminist sound practices resist closure. The repetition of names and refrains insists that mourning is ongoing, that justice remains unfinished. As the anthropologist Veena Das (2001) observes, repetition in post-traumatic expression keeps wounds open not for suffering's sake but for ethical remembrance. In Greece, the annual re-singing of these songs ensures that victims are not forgotten and that their stories continue to animate calls for reform.

6.3 Music as Infrastructure for Solidarity

Beyond symbolic protest, feminist music functions as a social infrastructure that supports long-term mobilisation (De Beukelaer, 2019). In a society where feminist organisations often lack institutional resources, songs provide a low-cost, high-impact means of community-building. They circulate through concerts, online playlists, school performances and even informal gatherings, carrying feminist discourse into spaces that formal activism may not reach. This is particularly evident in local choirs and youth groups who have adopted feminist songs into their repertoires, embedding gender awareness in community culture.

In this way, music serves as both affective glue and logistical network. It gathers people, sustains attention and redistributes resources. It also models egalitarian participation in that anyone can sing, hum or share a track, thus enacting the inclusive politics it advocates (Woodford, 2001). The act of communal singing, unhierarchical and embodied, mirrors the feminist ideal of collective empowerment.

6.4 Mobilisation Through Media: The Digital Echo

Digital media extend this mobilisation beyond physical gatherings, amplifying its reach. When a femicide case breaks, social media timelines in Greece quickly fill with posts quoting lyrics or sharing videos of feminist songs. This practice functions as an immediate *sonic memorial*, enabling users to express outrage and solidarity through the familiar language of music (Geismar, 2005).

Algorithms, often criticised for promoting distraction, here assist in diffusion. Trending songs reach users far outside feminist circles, turning passive listeners into potential allies. The emotional immediacy of sound, its ability to bypass linguistic and ideological barriers, allows these messages to travel where textual activism might not.

Moreover, digital remixes and covers of feminist songs contribute to the building of temporary communities united by feeling rather than formal affiliation. Each shared post becomes a micro-act of mobilisation, a node in a wider network of feminist empathy. The result is a participatory ecosystem in which music generates both awareness and belonging.

6.5 The Limits and Potentials of Sonic Activism

While the transformative potential of feminist music in Greece is evident, its limitations must also be acknowledged. Cultural activism operates within structural constraints. It can shift discourse and inspire action, but it cannot alone guarantee legal or institutional reform (Reed, 2019). The danger lies in the commodification or co-option of feminist sound. When powerful songs are absorbed into advertising, media soundtracks or state-sponsored events, their radical charge may dissipate.

Another risk is the aestheticisation of trauma. As feminist critics such as Catherine Clément (1994) and Susan Sontag (Furstenau, 2007) remind us, art that represents suffering can inadvertently turn it into spectacle. Greek feminist musicians tread this fine line by balancing emotional expressiveness with ethical restraint, refusing to reproduce violence sonically, focusing instead on solidarity and memory.

Yet these limitations do not negate the political efficacy of sound. Rather, they clarify its scope. Music does not replace legal reform. It accompanies, pressures and prepares the cultural ground for it (Canton, 2024). By transforming public sentiment, it shapes the conditions under which policy change becomes imaginable. The mass support for recognising femicide as a distinct legal category in Greece, for example, owes much to the emotional awareness cultivated by music and media.

Thus, even when it does not translate directly into legislative success, feminist sound activism alters the cultural climate in which politics unfolds. It nurtures a shared vocabulary of empathy, outrage and justice, affective prerequisites for systemic change.

6.6 From Sound to Action: The Moral Resonance of Empathy

The final movement from mourning to mobilisation depends on what might be called *moral resonance* (Nussbaum, 1997): the alignment of feeling and ethics that transforms empathy into collective will. Music, by its very nature, creates resonance: physical, emotional and social. When listeners feel vibrations in their bodies, they are reminded of interconnectedness, of the fact that harm to one resonates across many.

This embodied awareness is the foundation of feminist ethics. As Carol Gilligan (1982) and bell hooks (2000) have argued, care and empathy are not sentimental responses but political capacities that sustain community. In the Greek context, the shared experience of singing or listening to songs about femicide cultivates precisely this capacity. It teaches citizens to inhabit vulnerability without shame and to see in others' suffering a call to action.

The ethical demand of feminist music lies, then, in its insistence that *listening is not enough*. The affective power it generates must translate into structural commitment, whether that means supporting women's organisations, challenging misogynistic speech or lobbying for legislative reform. The echo of a song in one's mind after the music stops becomes a reminder that justice, too, must be sustained through repetition.

7. CONCLUSION: REWRITING SILENCE, RECLAIMING SOUND

Across the past decade, Greece has confronted a painful reckoning with the reality of femicide. The murders of women such as Eleni Topaloudi, Caroline Crouch, Garifallia Psarrakou and many others have not only exposed the persistence of gender-based violence but have also revealed the limits of the state, the law and the media in addressing it. Amid institutional inertia and cultural denial, music has emerged as one of the most powerful mediums through which Greek society confronts, narrates and resists femicide.

This chapter has traced the development of a distinctly feminist *sonic politics*, a movement that transforms mourning into mobilisation and private grief into public action (Hofman & Atanasovski, 2017). Through song, artists and listeners together have reclaimed sound as a space of solidarity, remembrance and defiance. The voices rising in protest, whether in concert halls, streets or digital platforms, have made femicide audible where it was once unspeakable, rewriting silence into resonance.

7.1 From the Margins to the Mainstream

One of the most striking aspects of this cultural transformation is how quickly feminist sound has moved from the margins of activism into the mainstream of Greek public life. When Orestis Dandtos and Ioulia Karapataki released 'Τακούνια για Καρφιά' ['Heels for Nails'], few could have predicted the extent to which it would circulate beyond feminist circles, becoming an anthem sung in schools, rallies and living rooms. The song's reach symbolises a broader shift: feminism, once treated as a niche or foreign import, now reverberates through the nation's most beloved cultural form.

This mainstreaming of feminist sound does not dilute its political potency. Rather, it extends its reach. It introduces feminist discourse into spaces that might resist overt activism: the radio station, the family gathering, the wedding playlist. By merging emotional appeal with aesthetic pleasure, music normalises feminist language and compassion, undermining the idea that discussions of gender violence belong solely to the political sphere.

Yet this mainstream success is also a reminder that the struggle for justice remains ongoing. As feminist scholars have long emphasised, cultural visibility is not the same as structural transformation (Dutta, 2011). The challenge is to ensure that the amplification of women's voices in song translates into tangible protections in law and everyday life. Music alone cannot legislate change. It can create the cultural atmosphere in which change becomes possible.

7.2 The Endurance of Feminist Memory

Music's unique power lies in its capacity to carry memory through time. While media cycles move rapidly from one tragedy to the next, songs linger. A melody heard months or years later can instantly reactivate a collective memory, reawakening the emotions and ethics tied to it. In this way, songs about femicide function as living archives (Tumilowicz, 2020), repositories of grief and resistance that keep victims' stories audible in the national consciousness.

The act of naming is particularly significant in this context. By transforming names into lyrics, music resists the erasure that often follows sensationalised news coverage. Each repetition of 'Eleni,' 'Caroline' or 'Garifallia' is a refusal of forgetfulness, a renewal of moral attention. As Judith Butler's (2009) notion of *grievability* suggests, to name is to acknowledge that a life was worthy of mourning and, by extension, worthy of justice.

Feminist musicians have thus become the archivists of affective history, keeping alive what official institutions too readily forget. Their songs ensure that each femicide becomes not an isolated event but part of a cumulative reckoning with patriarchy. The memory sustained in melody is not passive nostalgia but active vigilance.

7.3 Music as Feminist Praxis

This chapter has also argued that feminist music in Greece constitutes not merely cultural commentary but a *form of praxis*, a way of doing feminism through artistic and affective means. By transforming private pain into collective resonance, these songs perform a reorientation of emotion (Arcello, 2017). They redirect sorrow, anger and love towards political ends.

Through their lyrics, performances and digital circulation, feminist songs entail the potential to enact a pedagogy of empathy. They can teach listeners how to feel responsibly, how to transform emotion into an ethical relation. This pedagogy extends beyond explicit activism. It reshapes everyday listening habits. When an audience hums a refrain that insists 'for all of us,' it learns, even unconsciously, to perceive gender-based violence as a collective concern rather than a private misfortune.

In this sense, music functions as embodied theory (Pedwell, 2010). The affective dynamics explored by feminist scholars are not abstract ideas but lived experiences enacted in every shared performance. The feminist listener, like the feminist reader, becomes part of a community of feeling and understanding that exceeds linguistic articulation. Listening can mobilise a political practice.

7.4 The Global Resonance of Local Sound

Although the focus of this chapter has been Greece, the phenomenon it explores resonates globally. Feminist sonic activism connects Greek musicians and listeners to wider transnational movements – from Latin America's *Ni Una Menos* to Chile's *Un Violador En Tu Camino*, from Italy's protest ballads to the #MeToo soundscapes emerging across Europe. These parallels highlight how feminist struggles travel through rhythm and voice, creating a shared grammar of defiance that transcends language and borders.

At the same time, the Greek context contributes distinctively to this global resonance. The intertwining of *rebetiko's* lament traditions with contemporary genres like rap and *entechno* gives Greek feminist music a uniquely hybrid voice, rooted in history yet radically current. The Mediterranean soundscape, long associated with passion and melancholy, becomes here a vessel for political critique and moral renewal.

By situating feminist songs within this continuum, we recognise Greece not as a peripheral participant in global feminist culture but as an active site of innovation, where music mediates between the ancient and the contemporary, the local and the universal and between grief and action.

7.5 The Fragility and Power of Sound

Sound is ephemeral. It dissipates as soon as it is produced, leaving only vibration and memory. Yet this fragility is precisely what makes it powerful. Because it cannot be contained, sound moves through bodies, walls and air. It demands proximity, participation and repetition. Each performance of a feminist song reanimates its message, ensuring that it remains alive through use rather than preservation.

This ephemerality offers an important lesson for feminist politics. Just as sound must be continually produced to exist, justice must be continually enacted to endure. There is no final victory against patriarchy, only the ongoing resonance of voices refusing silence. The feminist soundscape of Greece reminds us that activism, like music, depends on rhythm of collective solidarity: persistence, return, echo.

7.6 Towards an Ethics of Resonance

The final insight to emerge from this exploration is an ethical one. Feminist music teaches that listening is a moral act (Morris, 1998). To listen is to accept responsibility, to be moved by the vulnerability of others, to allow resonance to change one's stance towards the world. In societies marked by systemic inequality, listening becomes an act of redistribution (Beausoleil, 2021). It shifts attention, empathy and care towards those most often unheard.

When a listener in Athens or Thessaloniki sings along to one of the songs discussed in Section 4 of this chapter, they are participating in *acoustic citizenship*, that is, the creation of community through shared sound. This citizenship is not granted by law but performed through resonance. It declares, in every refrain, that women's lives and voices matter.

Ultimately, the struggle against femicide in Greece is as much a struggle over sound as it is over law, over who speaks, who is heard and whose silence counts. In reclaiming sound, feminist musicians and activists have reclaimed the right to define public feeling, to turn lament into demand and to insist that the country's moral compass be tuned to the frequency of justice.

7.7 Closing Reflection

The story traced in this chapter – of grief transfigured into solidarity and silence rewritten through song – is one of heartbreak and hope. It shows how culture can become a site of resistance when formal institutions fail. The songs examined here are not merely artistic responses to tragedy; they are acts of civic intervention. They remind us that sound, at its core, is relational: it requires both a voice and an ear, both expression and attention.

In Greece's ongoing battle against gender-based violence, these songs ensure that the silence surrounding women's suffering will not return unchallenged. Their melodies carry the weight of remembrance and the promise of change. To sing, to share, to listen. These are not passive gestures but forms of participation in an unfinished movement towards equality.

If the history of Greek protest music has taught anything, it is that sound can outlast fear. In the echo of each feminist refrain, we hear a collective refusal: *no more silence, no more deaths, no more forgetting*. What begins as music becomes, finally, a moral imperative. A call that continues to reverberate, urging a society still learning how to listen more justly, more fully, and more loudly.

NOTES

1. Music composition by Giannis Ioannou and lyrics by Panos Stathogiannis.
2. New lyrics by Dimitris Athanasopoulos.
3. Original music composition by Vivir Quitana. Greek lyrics and adaptation by θηλυκότητες της Ανοιχτής Ορχήστρας (Femininities of the Open Orchestra).

REFERENCES

Abelson, M. J. (2014). Dangerous privilege: Trans men, masculinities, and changing perceptions of safety. *Sociological Forum*, *29*(3), 549–570.

Agarwal, B. (2015). The power of numbers in gender dynamics: Illustrations from community forestry groups. *Journal of Peasant Studies*, *42*(1), 1–20.

Ahmed, S. (2004). *The cultural politics of emotion*. Routledge.

Ahmed, S. (2017). *Living a feminist life*. Duke University Press.

Arcello, A. F. (2017). *Love in Action': The transformative role of emotion in writing and learning contexts* [Doctoral Thesis]. University of Wisconsin—Madison.

Asavei, M. A. (2019). The art and politics of imagination: Remembering mass violence against women. *Critical Review of International Social and Political Philosophy*, *22*(5), 618–636.

Avramopoulou, E. (2025). Burning issues, burned subjects: Cruel temporalities in the field of gender-based violence. *Journal of Greek Media & Culture*, *11*(1), 71–87.

Beausoleil, E. (2021). Listening to claims of structural injustice. In *Institutional transformations* (pp. 118–133). Routledge.

Bridgeman, J. (2013). Relational vulnerability, care and dependency. In *Vulnerabilities, care and family law* (pp. 199–215). Routledge.

Butler, J. (1999). *Gender trouble: Feminism and the subversion of identity*. Routledge.

Butler, J. (2009). *Frames of war: When is life grievable*? Verso Books.

Butler, J. (2015). *Notes toward a performative theory of assembly*. Harvard University Press.

Butler, J., & Athanasiou, A. (2013). *Dispossession: The performative in the political*. John Wiley & Sons.

Canton, W. (Ed.) (2024), *Sonic rebellions: Sound and social justice*. CRC Press.

Cayli, B. (2017). Victims and protest in a social space: Revisiting the sociology of emotions. *Emotion, Space and Society*, *22*, 61–70.

Chakravarty, D. (2013). *Going transnational': Politics of transnational feminist exchange and discourse in/between India and the United States* [Doctoral Thesis]. Arizona State University. https://www.proquest.com/openview/6f5b3634d597a10cbe2b074d41fc54f3/1?pq-origsite=gscholar&cbl=18750

Chaney, D. (1983). A symbolic mirror of ourselves: Civic ritual in mass society. *Media, Culture & Society*, *5*(2), 119–135.

Clément, C. (1994). *Syncope: The philosophy of rapture*. University of Minnesota Press.

Cowan, J. K. (1993). Politics, identity and popular music in contemporary Greece. In *Kampos: Cambridge papers in modern Greek* (pp. 1–22).

Czaszewicz, J. (2024). *Decolonizing the music industry: A case study of independent music Artists on TikTok* [Mater's thesis, Utrecht University]. Utrecht University Student Theses Repository Home. https://studenttheses.uu.nl/handle/20.500.12932/46409

Das, V. (Ed.) (2001), *Remaking a world: Violence, social suffering, and recovery*. University of California Press.

De Beukelaer, C. (2019). The social and built infrastructure of cultural policy: Between selective popular memory and future plans. *International Journal of Cultural Policy*, *25*(2), 140–153.

DeNora, T. (1995). The musical composition of social reality? Music, action and reflexivity. *The Sociological Review*, *43*(2), 295–315.

DeNora, T. (2000). *Music in everyday life*. Cambridge University Press.

Dutta, M. J. (2011). *Communicating social change: Structure, culture, and agency*. Routledge.

Economou, L. (2018). Sentiment, memory, and identity in Greek laiko music (1945–1967). In *Made in Greece* (pp. 17–27). Routledge.

Efthymiadou, M. (2025). Collage-making as ethnographic inquiry. *Teaching Anthropology*, *14*(2), 151–155.

EIGE. (n.d.). *Country profile for Greece.* https://eige.europa.eu/gender-based-violence/countries/greece?language_content_entity=en#:~:text=Women%20are%20disproportionately%20affected%20by%20intimate%20partner,by%20domestic%20perpetrators%20(24%20out%20of%2036. Accessed on September 10, 2025.

Erlmann, V. (2020). But what of the ethnographic ear? Anthropology, sound, and the senses. In *Hearing cultures* (pp. 1–20). Routledge.

Ertürk, Y. (2009). Towards a post-patriarchal gender order: Confronting the universality and the particularity of violence against women. *Sociologisk Forskning*, *46*(4), 61–70.

Flügel, P. (2018). Social-differentiation and self-differentiation: The Jaina concept of the individual and sociological individualisation-paradigms. *Max Weber Studies*, *18*(2), 212–273.

Frantzi, K. (2024). Topaloudi's legacy: Greek TV journalism and gender-based violence in the# MeToo era. *The International Journal of Interdisciplinary Social and Community Studies*, *19*(2), 109–130.

Fraser, N. (1990). Rethinking the public sphere: A contribution to the critique of actually existing democracy. *Social Text*, *25/26*, 56–80.

Furstenau, M. (2007). The ethics of seeing: Susan Sontag and visual culture studies. *Post Script*, *26*(2), 91–104.

Geismar, H. (2005). Building sites of memory: The ground zero sonic memorial sound walk. *Fabrications*, *15*(2), 1–13.

Gerasopoulos, V. (2020). The malleable and inevitable path of demonizing (sub) culture: The case of Greek Rebetiko. In *Crime and music* (pp. 247–269). Springer International Publishing.

Gilligan, C. (1982). *In a different voice: Psychological theory and women's development.* Harvard University Press.

Grammatikopoulou, C. (2025). Feminist networks of care in Greece. Practices of resistance from the streets to the screens. *Digital Geography and Society*, *8*. https://doi.org/10.1016/j.diggeo.2025.100113

Haroun, Y. (2024). Translation and politics. In *The routledge handbook of translation and sociology* (pp. 213–228). Routledge.

Highmore, B. (2011). Out of place: Unprofessional painting, Jacques Rancière, and the distribution of the sensible. In *Reading Rancière: Critical dissensus* (pp. 95–110). Continuum.

Hofman, A., & Atanasovski, S. (2017). Sonic memory interventions against politics of urban silencing. МузиколоГија/*Musicology*, *1*(22), 89–101.

Holst-Warhaft, G. (1998/2020). Rebetika: The double-descended deep songs of Greece. In *The passion of music and dance* (pp. 111–126). Routledge.

Holst-Warhaft, G. (2003). The female dervish and other shady ladies of the rebetika. In *Music and gender: Perspectives from the Mediterranean* (pp. 169–194).

hooks, b. (2000). *Feminism is for everybody: Passionate politics*. Pluto Press.

Ingleton, H. (2017). *Composing paradoxes feminist process in sound arts and experimental musics* [Doctoral dissertation, City, University of London]. City Research Online. https://openaccess.city.ac.uk/id/eprint/17510

Jameson, F. (2002). *A singular modernity: Essay on the ontology of the present*. Verso.

Johnson, J. (2019). Post-secular musicals in a post-truth world. In *The Routledge companion to the contemporary musical* (pp. 265–272). Routledge.

Karakasi, M. V., Nikolaidis, I., Fotou, E., Sapounas, A., Patounas, A., Sakka, S., Ntentopoulos, C., Pavlidis, P., & Voultsos, P. (2025). Emerging trends in intimate partner rape and marital/spousal rape during the biennium 2020 and 2021, including the Covid-19 pandemic in Greece. *Journal of Interpersonal Violence*, *40*(1–2), 370–396.

Kogiou, A. (2025). The effects of the Greek'Metoo'movement on representations of femicide in the news media and social media. *Envisioning the Future of Communication*, 2(1), 509–522.

Koureta, A., Gaganakis, M., Georgiadou, E., Bozikas, V. P., & Agorastos, A. (2025). Heterosexual intimate partner femicide: A narrative review of victim and perpetrator characteristics. *Brain Sciences*, *15*(6), 589.

Kourou, M., & Athanasiades, C. (2022). The portrayal of femicide in the Greek internet press. *Scientific Annals-School of Psychology AUTh*, *14*, 173–200.

Kouroutsidou, M., & Kakarouna, S. M. (2021). The phenomenon of femicide and the Greek experience. *European Journal of Humanities and Social Sciences*, *1*(5), 23–26.

Kyriakopoulou-Kollia, F. (2019). *A feminist criminological critique of aspects of the criminal justice system and the whole-system response towards female victims of intimate partner abuse* [Doctoral dissertation, Newcastle University]. University Repository. http://theses.ncl.ac.uk/jspui/handle/10443/4734

LaBelle, B. (2018). *Sonic agency: Sound and emergent forms of resistance.* Goldsmiths Press.

Lamas, M. (2011). *Feminism: Transmissions and retransmissions.* Springer.

Lehmann, H., Roth, H., & Schankweiler, K. (2019). Affective economy. In *Affective societies* (pp. 140–151). Routledge.

Lomazzi, V. (2023). The cultural roots of violence against women: Individual and institutional gender norms in 12 countries. *Social Sciences*, *12*(3). https://doi.org/10.3390/socsci12030117

Lopez, F. (2018). Between "Normalization" and spectacularization. Representing violence against women in TV crime series. *Journalism and Mass Communication*, *8*(6), 277–286.

Lorde, A. (1997). The uses of anger. *Women's Studies Quarterly*, *25*(1/2), 278–285.

Maricic, M., & Jeremic, V. (2024). Measuring gender equality in the European Union: Scrutinizing the gender equality index. *Statistica Applicata-Italian Journal of Applied Statistics.* https://doi.org/10.26398/IJAS.239

Matthews, S. (2001). Change and theory in Raymond Williams's structure of feeling. *Pretexts: Literary and Cultural Studies*, *10*(2), 179–194.

McGuire, J. T. (2025). Using typology to classify social movements: Feminism in two contexts. *The American Sociologist*, *56*(2), 373–387.

Mcteam. (2023, March 11). "Όλες απαντάμε αν αγγίξεις μία": Το τραγούδι-γροθιά κατά της έμφυλης βίας. *Marie Claire.* https://www.marieclaire.gr/art-lifestyle/oles-apantame-an-angixis-mia-to-tragoudi-grothia-kata-tis-emfilis-vias/

Michael, B. (2018). Introduction: Sonic spaces and places. In *The routledge companion to sound studies* (pp. 143–146). Routledge.

Mohanty, C. T. (2003). *Feminism without borders: Decolonising theory, practicing solidarity*. Duke University Press.

Morris, D. (1998). *Illness and culture in the postmodern age*. University of California Press.

Nikolaidou, I. (2025). *The raise of gender-based violence during the COVID-19 lockdown: A comparative study of GBV cases between Denmark and Greece*. [Mater's thesis, Linnaeus University]. Digitala Vetenskapliga Arkivet. https://www.diva-portal.org/smash/record.jsf?pid=diva2%3A1988016&dswid=-9042

Niraki, M. (2023, April). Gender-based violence and intimate partner violence in Greece during the COVID–19 pandemic. In *International conference on gender research* (pp. 287–XII). Academic Conferences International Limited.

Nussbaum, M. C. (1997). Capabilities and human rights. *Fordham Law Review*, *66*, 273–300.

Papacharissi, Z. (2015). *Affective publics: Sentiment, technology, and politics*. Oxford University Press.

Papadogiannis, N. (2014). A (trans) national emotional community? Greek political songs and the politicisation of Greek migrants in West Germany in the 1960s and early 1970s. *Contemporary European History*, *23*(4), 589–614.

Papadogiannis, N. (2015). *Militant around the clock?: Left-wing youth politics, leisure, and sexuality in post-dictatorship Greece, 1974-1981*. Berghahn Books.

Papagiannopoulou, M. (2022). *Gender-based Violence in the pandemic period*. Centre for Gender Studies.

Parks, E. S. (2018). *The ethics of listening: Creating space for sustainable dialogue*. Bloomsbury Publishing.

Pedwell, C. (2010). *Feminism, culture and embodied practice: The rhetorics of comparison*. Routledge.

Proust, V. (2025). Protest anthems as songs of mourning: Feminist activism through collective expressions of grief. *Howard Journal of Communications*, *36*(2), 160–175.

Ranjan, S. (2020). Domestic violence legislation in Greece: Analysis of penal mediation. *Women & Criminal Justice*, *30*(1), 42–68.

Reed, T. V. (2019). *The art of protest: Culture and activism from the civil rights movement to the present.* University of Minnesota Press.

Remoundou, N. (2022). Wronged bodies: Gendering human rights abuses in contemporary Greek poetry. *Law and Humanities*, *16*(1), 28–58.

Schwaber, E. (1981). Narcissism, self psychology, and the listening perspective. *Annual of Psychoanalysis*, *9*, 115–131.

Sonevytsky, M. (2016). The freak cabaret on the revolution stage: On the ambivalent politics of femininity, rurality, and nationalism in Ukrainian popular music. *Journal of Popular Music Studies*, *28*(3), 291–314.

Sonevytsky, M. (2019). *Wild music: Sound and sovereignty in Ukraine.* Wesleyan University Press.

Steiner, G. (1982). I. In lieu of A preface. *Salmagundi*, *58/59*, 4–9.

Stetz, L. (2022). *Transnational feminist data visualization mapping of artists' responses to violence against women* [Doctoral Thesis]. The Pennsylvania State University. ProQuest. https://www.proquest.com/openview/6844da37c50fba41fa3a45f133b6dc03/1?pq-origsite=gscholar&cbl=18750&diss=y

Stoever, J. L. (2016). *The sonic color line: Race and the cultural politics of listening.* NYU Press.

The TOC Team. (2025, January 2). *Άγιοι Ανάργυροι: Η 15χρονη που τραυματίστηκε από σοβάδες - 'Δεν θέλω να περνάω κάτω από μπαλκόνια'.* The TOC. https://www.thetoc.gr/koinwnia/article/agioi-anarguroi-sugklonizei-i-15xroni-pou-traumatistike-apo-sobades—den-thelo-na-pernao-kato-apo-mpalkonia/. Accessed on December 30, 2025.

Tragaki, D. (2009). *Rebetiko worlds.* Cambridge Scholars Publishing.

Tsioulakis, I. (2020). *Musicians in crisis: Working and playing in the Greek popular music industry.* Routledge.

Tumilowicz, A. (2020). *The living archives: Journeys through performance remains* [Doctoral Thesis]. New York University. https://www.proquest.com/openview/e53a25db8cc553f5434afda78e28d240/1?pq-origsite=gscholar&cbl=18750&diss=y

Webb, L. M., Allen, M. W., & Walker, K. L. (2002). Feminist pedagogy: Identifying basic principles. *Academic Exchange*, *6*(1), 67–72.

Woodford, P. G. (2001). Music, reason, democracy, and the construction of gender. *Journal of Aesthetic Education*, *35*(3), 73–86.

4

ECHOES OF JUSTICE: FEMINIST RESONANCE ACROSS SPAIN AND GREECE

ABSTRACT

This conclusion examines how feminist musical practices in Spain and Greece function as vital modes of witnessing, mourning and resistance in the face of femicide and gender-based violence. Drawing on parallel yet distinct national contexts, the book demonstrates that music operates as a political, ethical and affective practice that challenges institutional silences and supplements incomplete legal responses. In Spain, musical genealogies from María Jiménez to Rozalén intersect with memory politics and advanced, though uneven, legislative frameworks. In Greece, musical activism emerges amid inconsistent institutional protections and highly publicised cases that expose structural misogyny. Across both sites, music generates affective publics, sustains feminist counter-memory, enacts cultural citizenship and circulates within transnational feminist soundscapes shaped by Latin American movements. The conclusion also foregrounds tensions between cultural visibility and institutional change, the volatility of digital publics and the limits of affect, arguing that musical activism offers indispensable yet partial forms of justice beyond the law.

Keywords: Feminist musical activism; femicide; gender-based violence; affective publics; cultural and affective citizenship; feminist soundscapes; transnational feminism; memory; mourning

1. PURPOSE OF THE BOOK

This book began from a simple but unsettling question: what happens when the institutions entrusted with protecting women's lives prove inadequate, indifferent or hostile – and yet grief, anger and the demand for justice still insist on being heard? In Spain and Greece, as in many parts of the world, the answer has increasingly been: music speaks where law and politics fall short. Building on this premise, the volume examines how musical practices in Southern Europe have become crucial arenas for mourning, memory and resistance in the face of femicide and gender-based violence.

The introduction positioned Spain and Greece as parallel yet distinct sites within the geography of European gender politics. Both countries are post-authoritarian democracies with enduring patriarchal legacies; both have witnessed an escalation of gender-based killings since the late 1990s and in both countries, music has emerged as a privileged space where the demand for gender justice acquires sonic form. By juxtaposing these two contexts, the book does not seek to dissolve their differences, but to understand how sound, voice and listening become feminist tools in landscapes marked by uneven legal protections, institutional silences and resurgent anti-gender politics.

At its core, the book has two aims. First, it shows that feminist music in Spain and Greece actively shapes social change. Through songs, performances and urban genres such as feminist perreo and reggaetón, music reshapes public understandings of feminicide, mourning and justice, turning private pain into shared political concern. Second, the book situates these musical practices within a wider transnational feminist soundscape that links Southern Europe with movements across Latin America, from Ni una menos to 'Canción sin miedo' and their Mediterranean adaptations, showing how music circulates as testimony, archive and a catalyst for mobilisation.

2. CONTRIBUTIONS OF THE SPAIN AND GREECE CHAPTERS

Taken together, the two chapters offer a carefully contextualised and complementary account of how music has become a vital medium for confronting gender-based violence and femicides in Southern Europe. While Spain and Greece differ in their institutional landscapes and historical trajectories, both chapters illuminate the central role of music in shaping public understanding, collective mourning and feminist mobilisation against feminicide.

The Spain chapter demonstrates how musical practices have long been intertwined with feminist activism and the broader transformation of public discourse on gender-based violence. Anchored in the pivotal case of *Ana Orantes (1997)*, the chapter shows how her televised testimony and subsequent murder reshaped national debates by foregrounding memory, emotion and testimony as essential to recognising violence against women. The commemorative performance of '*La puerta violeta*' by Rozalén 25 years later exemplifies the continued capacity of music to operate simultaneously as homage and political intervention, keeping the urgency of remembrance and justice firmly in view. A major contribution of the Spanish analysis lies in its examination of the *legal and institutional developments* that have unfolded since the introduction of the Organic Law 1/2004. While Spain's legislative framework stands as a reference point in Europe, the chapter highlights its limits: feminicides persist, support infrastructures remain uneven and antifeminist backlash continues to challenge established protections. In this context, music emerges as a crucial site of cultural resistance, sustaining feminist narratives and public awareness where political and juridical mechanisms alone have not proved sufficient. The chapter also traces a rich **genealogy of feminist musical expression**, beginning with the defiant rumba of *María Jiménez's* 'Se acabó' and extending through the feminist soundscapes of the 8M mobilisations, contemporary singer–songwriters and digital musical practices. This genealogy shows how music in Spain has consistently provided a platform for denouncing impunity, articulating resistance and building intergenerational feminist communities.

The chapter on Greece offers a parallel yet distinct contribution by situating musical activism within a context where institutional responses to femicides and gender-based violence remain inconsistent. Rather than focusing on long-term memory politics, the Greek analysis centres on the *contemporary landscape of femicide*, foregrounding cases such as *Eleni Topaloudi (2018)* and *Caroline Crouch (2021)*. These highly publicised murders revealed entrenched patterns of institutional neglect, cultural misogyny and victim-blaming that shaped both public discourse and legal processes. Through detailed contextualisation, the chapter shows how these cases became catalysts for national reckoning. Another significant contribution lies in the chapter's examination of the *legal and institutional gaps* that continue to shape gender-based violence in Greece. Despite the ratification of the Istanbul Convention, femicide remains absent as a distinct legal category, and support services for survivors are often under-resourced. This context helps explain why cultural expression – particularly music – has taken on heightened importance in efforts to make gendered violence visible and to hold institutions to account. The chapter also offers a nuanced analysis of *media representations*, showing how Greek mainstream media often reproduce harmful stereotypes, scrutinising victims' personal lives or framing perpetrators as emotionally unstable. Against this backdrop, feminist digital activism has created alternative platforms where victims are named, honoured and situated within broader patterns of structural violence. The central contribution of the Greek chapter lies in its exploration of *musical responses* to feminicide. Through case studies such as the Greek adaptation of '*Canción sin miedo*' ['Όλες απαντάμε αν αγγίξεις μία'], songs dedicated to Eleni Topaloudi and other compositions addressing femicides, the chapter demonstrates how music transforms mourning into mobilisation. These musical works function as elegies, protests and civic interventions that name victims, denounce institutional failings and invite listeners into communities of collective witnessing. They broaden the space of political expression beyond juridical or parliamentary arenas and into the emotional and affective registers that shape civic life.

A key contribution across both chapters is their focus on music as a form of justice. In Spain, the chapter shows how songs name victims, counter erasure and give visibility to experiences often marginalised by institutions. Music becomes a living archive where loss is acknowledged, and collective memory is sustained. In Greece, where legal recognition is limited and institutional responses are uneven, music similarly acts as a compensatory form of justice. It preserves victims' stories and challenges sensationalist or distorting narratives. Together, the chapters demonstrate how artistic expression supports feminist activism and shapes collective understandings of gendered violence, offering forms of justice that extend beyond formal institutions.

3. SHARED ANALYTICAL FRAMEWORK

Although the chapters on Spain and Greece examine different historical and institutional contexts, they share a common analytical approach. Both understand sound, affect and collective listening as central to contemporary feminist responses to femicide and gender-based violence. Rather than treating music as mere cultural expression, the book approaches it as a political and ethical practice that shapes how violence is recognised and resisted.

A first point of convergence is the idea that mourning is political. Drawing on Judith Butler's notion of grievability, both chapters show that some victims are publicly recognised while others are overlooked. Music helps counter this imbalance by naming women killed by men and by creating spaces of collective mourning. Whether in Spanish tributes to Ana Orantes or Greek performances honouring Eleni Topaloudi and Caroline Crouch, songs challenge silence and insist on public recognition. A second shared strand is the role of affect in feminist mobilisation. Following Sara Ahmed's work, both chapters show how emotions such as grief, anger and hope circulate through musical performance and listening. These emotions form what Zizi Papacharissi calls affective publics – communities that understand violence as part of a broader pattern rather than isolated events. Music becomes a way to organise and politicise feelings that drive feminist action. A third area of overlap is the idea of cultural and affective citizenship. Drawing on sound studies, the chapters argue that listening can be a form of civic participation. Songs create spaces where marginalised voices are heard – what Nancy Fraser terms counter-publics. Through singing, chanting, sharing or streaming, listeners enact forms of feminist citizenship that extend beyond formal institutions. This is particularly visible in Greece, where gaps in legal recognition make cultural expressions even more important. A fourth connection is their understanding of music as a site of memory work. This is more explicit in the Spanish chapter, which draws on Elizabeth Jelin and Marianne Hirsch. Music helps transmit memory and allows listeners to engage with losses they did not directly experience. In Spain, this draws on a longer tradition of post-dictatorship memory politics; in Greece, it emerges more directly from present struggles. In both cases, music sustains what the introduction describes as a feminist soundscape in which past and present forms of violence are narrated and challenged. A fifth shared dimension is the idea of justice beyond the law. Both chapters point to the limits of institutional responses: justice is often slow, uneven or incomplete. Music does not replace legal accountability, but it can supplement it by offering recognition, remembrance and communal healing. It helps create the emotional and moral conditions that make institutional change possible. Finally, the framework is transnational. Feminist musical repertoires travel across borders creating shared grammars of grief and resistance. This allows the book to trace how feminist ideas move, resonate and take on new meanings across different cultural contexts.

4. TENSIONS, LIMITS AND THE WORK OF JUSTICE

Despite the transformative potential of feminist musical practices in both Spain and Greece, the book also highlights several tensions and limits that shape what music can – and cannot – achieve in the struggle against feminicide. These limits do not diminish the political significance of music; rather, they reveal the complex terrain in which cultural and institutional forms of justice intersect.

One persistent tension lies in the gap between cultural visibility and institutional change. In Spain, decades of feminist mobilisation and rich musical engagement coexist with the continued presence of feminicides despite an advanced legislative framework. Music may amplify feminist critiques and sustain public attention, but it cannot ensure consistent implementation of policies or prevent institutional failures such as inadequate protection measures or uneven judicial responses. In Greece, this tension appears differently: music often fills the silence left by the absence of femicide as a legal category and by under-resourced support structures. While musical activism can raise awareness and mobilise affect, its impact remains limited without corresponding legal and institutional reform. Another tension concerns the ambivalent role of media and digital platforms. Feminist songs circulate widely online, generating affective publics and supporting rapid mobilisation, yet the same environments often reproduce misogynistic or sensationalist narratives. In both countries, musical interventions move through contested digital and media ecosystems in which feminist messages may challenge dominant narratives but also risk distortion, trivialisation or co-option. A further tension arises from the limits of affect as a political resource. Songs frequently surge in influence following particularly visible feminicides, but emotional energy alone cannot sustain long-term structural change. Without institutional mechanisms to build on these moments, musical activism can become episodic – powerful in the immediate aftermath yet vulnerable to dissipation over time. Finally, the book notes the delicate balance between recognising music as a powerful cultural force and avoiding the romanticisation of cultural resistance. As feminist messages enter commercial circuits or popular genres, they may gain wider audiences but also risk losing political clarity. Music can name victims, create solidarity and keep memory alive, but it cannot directly prosecute perpetrators, reform institutions or ensure protection for women at risk. Cultural justice is essential yet incomplete and must operate alongside robust legal and institutional reforms.

In the end, the volume shows that feminist musical activism in Spain and Greece is not merely expressive but world-making. Music gathers communities, sustains memory and keeps the demand for justice resonant when institutional responses waver. As these soundscapes continue to evolve, they invite us to listen with care, to recognise violence where it is often muted and to imagine futures in which justice is enacted in law, shared and carried in collective resonance.

ABOUT THE AUTHOR

Angelos Bollas is an independent scholar. His research focuses on sociology, cultural studies and education. He has authored and edited eight books including *Contemporary Irish Masculinities* (Routledge, 2024), *Sexualised Governmentalities* (Springer, 2024), *Fashionable Queerness* (Emerald, 2024), *HIV/AIDS in Memory, Culture and Society* (Palgrave Macmillan, 2024 with Alicia Castillo Villanueva), *The Routledge Companion to Sally Rooney* (Routledge, 2025), *Designing Curricula for Student Autonomy and Engagement* (Springer, 2026 with Cathryn Bennett), *Voices of Resistance* (Emerald, 2026 with Alicia Castillo Villanueva) and *Health and Care in Crisis in Sally Rooney's Literary Universe* (Palgrave Macmillan, 2026 with Elsa Adá-Hernández). Angelos has a PhD in Cultural Studies, five Master's degrees and two Bachelor's degrees. He is currently studying for his third Bachelor's degree in Philosophy and is a Learning Experience Designer at the Royal College of Physicians of Ireland.

Alicia Castillo Villanueva is an Associate Professor of Gender and Hispanic Studies at Dublin City University. Her research examines gender-based violence, memory politics and feminist cultural practices in contemporary Spain and other post-dictatorial societies. She has written widely on trauma, postmemory, silence and feminist forms of justice. She is a co-editor of *HIV/AIDS in Memory, Culture and Society* (Palgrave, 2024), *New Approaches to Translation, Conflict and Memory: Narratives of the Spanish Civil War and the Dictatorship* (Palgrave, 2019), and is currently editing *The Routledge Handbook of Gender, Memory, and Violence in the Hispanic World*. Her recent work explores postmemory, the ethics of repair and the role of culture and sound in feminist responses to gender-based violence.